SAVOR *the* SEASONS

THIRD IN THE SERIES

FROM

THE JUNIOR LEAGUE OF TAMPA

CULINARY COLLECTION

JUNIOR
LEAGUE
of TAMPA
*Culinary
Collection*

CREATORS OF THE GASPARILLA COOKBOOK, A TASTE OF TAMPA,
TAMPA TREASURES, THE LIFE OF THE PARTY, AND EVERYDAY FEASTS

To purchase copies of *Savor the Seasons*,
visit us online at www.jltampa.org, complete the order form in the back of this book,
or call The Junior League of Tampa at 813-254-1734, extension 502.

An Invitation to Celebrate

Each of us enjoys distinct memories of our favorite holiday.
From an elegant Thanksgiving dinner to a Halloween street party on the cul-de-sac,
our yearly celebrations are central to our lives. Unique traditions warm our hearts
as we savor them with our families, friends, and communities.

Savor the Seasons, Volume 3 of The Junior League of Tampa Culinary Collection,
invites you to join us on a year-round tour of seasonal menus,
festive flavors, and traditions with a twist.

Holidays renew and revitalize us, providing welcome time to relax and reconnect
with those we hold dear. They also offer wonderful occasions to experience
culinary customs and create new ones.

We would like to share some of our time-honored traditions with you and your family.
Savor the Seasons brings together a cornucopia of recipes and menus to infuse
new life into your holiday gatherings. Try our twists on classics, like a waterfront
salute to America barbecue, a Champagne brunch to ring in the New Year,
and a Valentine's dinner under the stars.

Holiday seasons also bring opportunities to help those around us
who are enduring difficult times. Here at The Junior League of Tampa,
we incorporate our holiday traditions into our community projects.
This book presents a special glimpse into the unique ways we
savor the seasons with children and families in the Tampa Bay area.

As you feast your eyes on our collection of recipes, we hope each page
will reveal fresh ideas for making your celebrations both meaningful and memorable.

—*Savor the Seasons Committee*

SAVOR *the* SEASONS

THE JUNIOR LEAGUE OF TAMPA
Culinary Collection

SAVOR *the* SEASONS

Volume 3 of The Junior League of Tampa Culinary Collection

The Junior League of Tampa, Inc., is an organization of women committed to
promoting voluntarism, developing the potential of women, and improving communities
through effective action and leadership of trained volunteers. Its purpose
is exclusively educational and charitable.

Proceeds from the sale of this cookbook will be reinvested in the community
through The Junior League of Tampa projects.

The Junior League of Tampa, Inc.
87 Columbia Drive
Tampa, Florida 33606
813-254-1734

ISBN-10: 0-9609556-5-8
ISBN-13: 978-0-9609556-5-7
Library of Congress Control Number: 2006925637
Edited, Designed, and Manufactured by
Favorite Recipes® Press

FRP™

P.O. Box 305142
Nashville, Tennessee 37230
800-358-0560

Book Design: David Malone
Art Director: Steve Newman
Project Editor: Tanis Westbrook

Manufactured in the United States of America
First Printing 2007
20,000 copies

This cookbook is a collection of favorite recipes,
which are not necessarily original recipes.

Major Contributors

Special thanks to our major contributors for their gracious support of
Savor *the* Seasons

CORPORATE SPONSOR

PUBLIX SUPER MARKETS
CHARITIES

Cookbook Photography— © Robert Adamo

Food Stylist—Kristie Salzer

Set Stylist—Tricia T. Smedley

Florist—The Potting Shed, Julian K. Cunningham, designer

The Junior League of Tampa Culinary Collection Logo—
Atlas Advertising and Design, Christy Atlas

Cookbook Development Committee

Chairman
Taylour Smedley-Shimkus

Communications Coordinator
Jessica McIntyre

Copywriting/Editing
Kimberly French, Corey Poe

Photography
Laura Muldoon, Kristina Smallwood

Recipe Collection
Charlene Bleakley, Irene Quisenberry

Recipe Testing
Allison Belcher, Stacey Bessone, Margaret A. Forehand

Kathleen Patterson Lopez, President 2005–2006

Pamela Childers Divers, President 2006–2007

COVER PHOTO SPONSORSHIPS

FRONT COVER IMAGE
*The front cover photograph was
generously underwritten by
Mary Lee Nunnally Farrior.*

BACK COVER IMAGE
*The back cover photograph was
generously underwritten by
Laura Mickler Bentley.*

SPECIAL THANKS

*A cookbook is a collaboration of many people. To all those listed here,
we thank you sincerely for your part in this endeavor. We have made every effort
to express our gratitude to everyone who has touched this project. If we have
inadvertently left out your name, please accept our sincere apologies.*

*To the families who so graciously gave us access to their
beautiful homes for the photos in this cookbook:*

David and Elizabeth Kennedy
Richard and Suzanne Moss
Charles and Corey Poe
Joseph and Mary Gayle Wessel

*To the businesses that allowed us access to props and
settings for the photographs in this cookbook:*

Alvin Magnon Jewelers
Magnolia
Villa Rosa Distinctive Linens & Bath Shop

Menu Photo Sponsorships

Ring in the New Year
This photograph was generously underwritten by Poe Financial Group.

From the Heart
This photograph was generously underwritten by Terrie Dodson and Mark Caldevilla.

Spring Tea
This photograph was generously underwritten by Bettie Twomey Bode and Kay Bode.

Salute to America
This photograph was generously underwritten by Betsy and Drew Graham.

Halloween Street Party
This photograph was generously underwritten by Sally S. Hill, Diana Brannon Shuler, and Peninsular Paper Company, Inc.

Giving Thanks
This photograph was generously underwritten by Junior League of Tampa Presidents Susan O'Neal Thompson (2004–2005), Kathleen Patterson Lopez (2005–2006), Pamela Childers Divers (2006–2007), and Susan Lem Touchton (2007–2008).

Holiday Tapas
This photograph was generously underwritten by Past Junior League of Tampa Cookbook Chairs Ginny Haelsig, Lou P. Hatton, Marie H. Preston, and Kathy Stephens.

WOMEN BUILDING BETTER COMMUNITIES

 The Junior League of Tampa cookbooks have always served as a legacy, an investment of time and tradition, handed from one generation to another, from our community to yours. But more than that, The Junior League of Tampa cookbooks are an investment in the foundation of our community.

Since 1926, the volunteers in our organization have shared their time, talent, and treasures with the city of Tampa. Here is a glimpse of some of the projects and organizations that we have been proud to support through volunteer hours and money raised through fund-raisers, including the sale of our cookbooks.

Academy Preparatory Center of Tampa
Alpha House, A Home for Pregnant Women
Baby Bungalow, An Early Childhood Resource and Support Center
Child Abuse Task Force
Children's Cancer Center
Children's Literacy Project
Drug Abuse Comprehensive Coordinating Office
FunBook/FunCart for Hospitalized Children
Guardian Ad Litem
Habitat for Humanity
Hillsborough Kids Inc./Kids Connect Special Needs Adoption Events
H. Lee Moffitt Hospital & Cancer Research Institute
Immunization Promotion Campaign
Hillsborough Hospice Circle of Love Bereavement Camp
Lowry Park Zoo Educational Program for Schoolchildren
Love Bundles
Mary Lee's House
Metropolitan Ministries Day Care Center
Minority Youth Leadership Program for Girls
MORE Health, An Education Program for Schoolchildren
PACE Center for Girls
Tampa Bay Performing Arts Center
Tampa General Hospital Sunshine House/Ronald McDonald House
Kid City, The Children's Museum of Tampa
The Spring of Tampa Bay, A Domestic Violence Shelter
Thumbs Up for Child Safety
YMCA Day Care Resource and Referral Service

CONTENTS

CELEBRATIONS

RING IN THE NEW YEAR

A vibrant Champagne brunch creates the perfect setting to welcome a New Year with family and close friends. Our menu offers some wonderful dishes you can prepare ahead of time so your morning is more relaxed. Overnight French Toast, Bacon and Leek Quiche, Eggnog Tea Bread, and Pineapple Casserole can be assembled the day before, refrigerated, and baked just before serving. Marinated Asparagus with Cherry Tomatoes is a simple recipe that adds both color and freshness to the table. Add some sparkle to your celebration with confetti, party hats, and horns held over from your midnight celebration. As you gather to recap the last year or talk about seasons to come, begin with a traditional New Year's toast.

Here's to the year past and friends who have left us.
Here's to the present and the friends who are here.
Here's to the New Year and the new friends who
will join us.
—UNKNOWN

MENU

OVERNIGHT FRENCH TOAST

BACON AND LEEK QUICHE

EGGNOG TEA BREAD

MARINATED ASPARAGUS
WITH CHERRY TOMATOES

PINEAPPLE CASSEROLE

HERE ARE SOME OTHER MERRY WAYS TO RING IN THE NEW YEAR WITH YOUR GUESTS:

LUCKY PEAS. A spoonful of black-eyed peas or a serving of Hoppin' John on New Year's Day brings good luck, according to southern tradition. Some families hide a silver coin in the dish—the person who receives a serving with the coin has the best luck of the year.

NEW YEAR, NEW RESOLUTIONS. Enlist everyone at the table to name one personal or professional goal for the year and state it aloud. Verbalizing goals and resolutions can give them more meaning.

SHOULD OLD ACQUAINTANCE BE FORGOT? Another idea is to have each guest recount a favorite memory, moment, or event from the year.

Most importantly, enjoy this special time together as an opportunity to relax and reconnect with each other.

FROM THE HEART

Everyone loves a meaningful celebration. Whether you're honoring your beloved with a birthday, anniversary, or Valentine's Day dinner, be sure to add a personal touch to make the evening memorable. A private table on the patio with a backdrop of twinkle lights can heighten the romanticism.

TRY THESE UNIQUE WAYS TO INFUSE SENTIMENT AND HUMOR INTO YOUR SPECIAL OCCASION.

MENU

GRAPEFRUIT AND BLUE CHEESE
SALAD WITH TOASTED WALNUTS

ROASTED BEEF TENDERLOIN WITH
BRANDY CREAM SAUCE

HERB-ROASTED FINGERLING
POTATOES WITH CAVIAR

GLAZED CARROTS

WARM RASPBERRY
CHOCOLATE CAKE

VALENTINE ADVENTURES. Flowers and chocolates are nice, but Valentine gifts from the heart mean so much more.

- Decorate the table with paper hearts that have sayings or special memories.
- Top off the evening with an original ode, or borrow one from your favorite poet.
- Send your Valentine on a scavenger hunt through the house to find a special gift.

ANNIVERSARY ARCHIVES. Though custom calls for gifts of silver or gold, why not add a twist to your anniversary tradition?

- Write each other heartfelt letters to save in a special keepsake box. Each year you can look back at wonderful memories and appreciate your marriage all the more.
- Watch your wedding video or look at your wedding album together.
- Recreate a meal from your honeymoon or favorite vacation.
- Sign up for dance, tennis, or golf lessons— anything you can enjoy together.

SHARING VALENTINE'S DAY WITH CHILDREN:
- Have a family fondue party.
- Treat your kids to strawberries and sparkling juice.
- Decorate heart-shaped cookies.

TIME TO TOAST. A birthday dinner offers the perfect occasion for a toast. Follow these etiquette guidelines when toasting:
- The host or hostess proposes the first toast.
- The toaster always stands and raises a glass at the conclusion.
- The person being toasted should remain seated and refrain from drinking during the toast.

SPRING TEA

With warm weather and flowers abloom, spring is the season to rediscover the beauty of the outdoors. A lovely table set in a sun-dappled garden welcomes a host of spring celebrations, from Easter to Mother's Day.

EASTER EGGSTRAVAGANZA. As a backdrop to your Easter egg hunt, set a table on the patio with bite-size morsels and traditional tea for adults to enjoy while children search the yard with their baskets. Include a special plate with Easter cookies and a tray of apple juice in small cups for the children.

QUEEN MUM. Spoil Mom with a lovely Mother's Day tea, complete with fine china and crisp linens. A mouthwatering selection of tea sandwiches and luscious sweets on three-tiered servers, a beautiful flower arrangement, and steaming pots of tea will help you treat her like a true queen.

SPRING SHOWERS. An afternoon tea party is a wonderful alternative to the traditional baby shower for the mother-to-be with a menu that includes hot and cold teas, sweet treats, and savory sandwiches.

MENU

CRANBERRY WALNUT SCONES WITH
HONEY ORANGE CREAM

SESAME-CRUSTED CHICKEN SALAD
TEA SANDWICHES

TOASTED BRIE CHICKEN
TEA SANDWICHES

SUMMERTIME MELON SALAD

PEACH RASPBERRY TRIFLE

ZIPPY STRAWBERRY ICED TEA

TEDDY BEAR TEA. One is never too young to learn how to give to others or support a cause. Host a Mother-Daughter tea for your friends, asking each child to bring a teddy bear or gift to be donated to a local shelter. Make this tea an annual event and a memory your child will cherish.

TIPS FOR TAKING TEA:

• A great idea for place cards at the table is to remove the tags from tea bags, replace them with small handwritten name tags, and put a teabag in an empty cup at each guest's place.

• Ask each guest to bring a vintage teacup and saucer. Not only will the variety of teacups liven up your table setting, but the stories behind them will add interest to the typical afternoon chat.

• If you like your tea a little on the sweet side, indulge in amber sugar crystals—an all-natural alternative to granulated sugar. The subtle caramel flavor of these amber nuggets adds just the right amount of sweetness.

• For a traditional British tea, serve at four or five o'clock with cookies, small sandwiches, breads, or cakes. The Brits enjoy their tea with sugar and milk.

SALUTE TO AMERICA

Summer cookouts bring Americans together to honor our great nation and the sacrifices of many for our freedom. At the pinnacle of patriotic celebrations is July Fourth, a time for fireworks, barbecues, and good old-fashioned fun.

Make your patriotic celebration sizzle with a lively spread by the pool, at the water's edge, or in your backyard with fresh meats and vegetables grilling nearby. We've assembled some wonderful selections to spark your salute to America.

Welcome the distinctive summer flavors of Spicy Melon Salsa complemented by refreshing Pomegranate Margaritas to cool your guests. Sweet and Spicy Summer Ribs hot off the grill served with Blue Cheese Onions and Broccoli-Orange Salad are sure to tantalize your taste buds. Freshly grilled vegetables add zest to any patriotic barbecue. Soak vegetables in cold water before grilling to prevent dehydration. Avoid small pieces that could fall through the grill, or opt for skewers to hold them together.

MENU

Spicy Melon Salsa

Sweet and Spicy Summer Ribs

Broccoli-Orange Salad

Brownie Mint Squares

Pomegranate Margaritas

Follow these guidelines for perfect veggie-grilling:

Zucchini/Squash: Cut into long pieces about one-half inch thick, or slice in half. Brush lightly with olive oil; add salt and pepper to taste. Grill for two to three minutes per side.

Corn: Use fresh corn in its full husk. Pull back the husk (keep it attached), and remove as much of the silk as possible. Soak the corn in cold water for thirty minutes or more; then dry, brush with melted butter, and pull the husk back over the corn, twisting its end. Place the corn (still in the husk) on a medium-hot grill. Grill for five to seven minutes, turning occasionally. Serve with melted butter, salt, pepper, and other seasonings to taste.

After your cookout, bring a cooler of drinks and desserts to enjoy your community's dazzling display of red, white, and blue fireworks.

HALLOWEEN STREET PARTY

The spookiest holiday of the year calls for carved pumpkins, haunted houses, and sinful sweets. Whether it's our choice of costume or the way we decorate our homes, Halloween brings out the creative child in all of us. Each year many of us look forward to summoning our neighbors for a ghoulishly good time.

At our Halloween Street Party, the families bring gruesome treats and bloody cocktails to share, the children unveil a spectrum of costume creations, and the evening gets off to a spirited start. To add ghostly ambience, fill your lawn with glowing luminaries, spooky jack-o'-lanterns, and giant, creepy-crawly spiders.

Set out a spread that would make Frankenstein proud, including Best-Ever Gingersnaps with Pumpkin Dip and wickedly good White Chocolate Party Mix. If there's a chill in the air, warm up your guests with Turkey Chipotle Chili and Hot Mulled Cider. We're sure the kids will love to get their hands in our Devilishly Delicious Dirt dessert.

MENU

TURKEY CHIPOTLE CHILI

GREEN CHILE AND
CHEDDAR CORN BREAD

BEST-EVER GINGERSNAPS
WITH PUMPKIN DIP

WHITE CHOCOLATE PARTY MIX

DEVILISHLY DELICIOUS DIRT

HOT MULLED CIDER

TRY THESE FRIGHT-FILLED IDEAS TO LIVEN UP THE DEADLIEST OF CELEBRATIONS:

• If your party is before Halloween, host a pumpkin carving contest with prizes for the most original, funniest, and scariest creations.

• Print bewitching bottle labels with clever names like Sick Cider or Carnal Cabernet on adhesive-backed paper, and press onto bottles to make libations truly your own creepy concoctions.

• Fill a darkened room with blindfolded guests, and have them reach into bowls containing spaghetti or peeled grapes. Their imaginations will run wild with the possibility of feeling worms, snakes, or eyeballs.

• For older children, few things invoke bone-chilling fright quite like a good old-fashioned ghost story in a haunted house. For maximum impact, hide a compatriot outside the house; when the tale reaches a crucial scary section, signal him to bang on windowpanes, jump out from a darkened corner, or cue mysterious wails from a CD player.

GIVING THANKS

Thanksgiving brings families and friends together to count their blessings over a bountiful feast. At the heart and hearth of every Thanksgiving dinner are dishes steeped in tradition.

Whether your gathering includes a group of close friends or generations of relatives, we encourage you to carry on meaningful customs and family recipes. Yet we also challenge you to add a twist to the traditional fare. Surprise your guests by putting the pumpkin in a divine Curried Pumpkin Crab Bisque and the cranberries in a sweet Apple Cranberry Pie.

HERE ARE SOME HELPFUL PREPARATION AND SERVING TIPS FOR MAKING YOUR THANKSGIVING FEAST DELIGHTFUL AND DELICIOUS.

TURKEY TIPS:

- If you're cooking for a large party, you'll need a big turkey—fifteen to twenty pounds. A good rule of thumb is to figure one and one-half pounds for each person. Smaller turkeys—twelve pounds or less—have a smaller meat-to-bone ratio, so allow two pounds per person.

MENU
CURRIED PUMPKIN CRAB BISQUE
SWEET POTATO SOUFFLÉ WITH PECAN STREUSEL
NOUVEAU HOLIDAY GREEN BEANS
APPLE WALNUT DRESSING
SMOKED TURKEY
FRUITED HOLIDAY COMPOTE
APPLE CRANBERRY PIE

- The best way to thaw a turkey is to place it in the coldest part of the refrigerator, allowing five hours of defrosting time for every pound.

GRAVY TIPS:

- If the gravy is doughy-tasting, make sure the flour has been thoroughly cooked. Once the flour has been added to the pan drippings, remember to whisk constantly while the mixture cooks until it turns a deep golden brown.

- If the gravy tastes like flour when you're almost finished, turn up the heat to maintain a rapid simmer for several minutes; then thin it again with more stock or water if necessary.

- If the gravy is too thin, reduce it by simmering over medium-high heat. If it's still too thin, make a paste of equal parts flour and softened unsalted butter, and add it a little at a time, whisking constantly, until the gravy thickens.

When setting your Thanksgiving table, place five kernels of corn above each plate. At the beginning of the meal, give each person at the table an opportunity to name five things for which he or she is thankful.

HOLIDAY TAPAS

The month of December presents a flurry of opportunities to celebrate the season. Why not plan a holiday party with a creative theme? The wonderful Spanish influences of Tampa make tapas, delicious little Spanish dishes, a natural choice for a unique culinary experience.

A tapas menu gives you the freedom to build an entire meal around dishes your guests will enjoy. It's an easy, affordable way to feast on a great combination of little dishes packed with big flavors.

TAPAS OFFER A WIDE RANGE OF POSSIBILITIES FOR HOME ENTERTAINING:

- Tapas are generally served in small portions and are meant to be eaten quickly and easily.
- There are no rules when serving tapas—they can be warm or cold and may include meat, fish, chicken, or vegetables.

MENU

SPANISH MEATBALLS

CEVICHE COCKTAIL

SKIRT STEAK WITH CHIMICHURRI

TOASTED PARMESAN ZUCCHINI

MELON MANCHEGO WRAPS

GUAVA RUM CHEESECAKE

CAVA COCKTAIL

- The number and variety of tapas you serve depends on the type of party you're having—three or four tapas are best for a handful of guests, while a large open house calls for at least ten different tapas.
- Plates and utensils may be provided or not, depending on the types of tapas served and the size of the party.
- In general, tapas that require forks and plates may be better suited for smaller parties, while tapas that can be picked up with fingers or wooden picks are more appropriate for larger parties.

The flexibility of a tapas menu makes it the perfect option for a festive holiday gathering. Our colorful menu includes just the right flavors to help your guests truly savor the holiday season—dishes like Ceviche Cocktail, Skirt Steak with Chimichurri, and Melon Manchego Wraps.

OPENERS

CEVICHE COCKTAIL

*This Spanish specialty is a fabulous seafood tapa served with chips or
a salad. To leave an impression, serve in a martini glass.*

1/3 to 1/2 pound fresh snapper or
sea bass, cut into 1/2×2-inch strips
1/3 pound fresh bay scallops
1/3 pound fresh shrimp, peeled,
deveined and chopped
1 red or purple onion, thinly sliced
1 yellow onion, thinly sliced
3 or 4 scallions, sliced on the bias
2 or 3 plum tomatoes,
seeded and chopped
2 or 3 garlic cloves, minced

1 or 2 jalapeño chiles, seeded
and minced
1 tablespoon minced fresh cilantro
Juice of 10 to 12 limes
Kosher salt and pepper to taste
1 avocado, cut into cubes
Lime wedges
Avocado cubes
Cherry tomatoes, halved
Tortilla chips
Lettuce leaves (optional)

Combine the snapper, scallops, shrimp, red onion, yellow onion, scallions, tomatoes, garlic,
jalapeños, cilantro, lime juice, salt and pepper in a large bowl and mix well. Or, combine in a large
sealable plastic bag. Chill, tightly covered, for 4 hours or longer. Add the avocado and toss gently to
combine. Chill, tightly covered, for 30 minutes. Spoon the mixture into martini glasses and garnish
with lime wedges, avocado cubes and cherry tomato halves threaded onto appetizer picks. Serve with
tortilla chips. Or, line a serving bowl with lettuce leaves and spoon the ceviche over the top.

Yield: 6 to 8 servings

ENTERTAINING TIP

If you are not serving dinner at your gathering, be sure to prepare

plenty of appetizers and desserts to keep your guests full and happy.

Assume eight to ten appetizers, including dessert per person.

HOT SHRIMP AND AVOCADO

*Outstanding! Just the right blend of curried shrimp and mellow avocado makes
this a wonderful appetizer, meal, or salad. We recommend using ripe Haas avocados
that are slightly soft to the touch and free of bruises.*

1 tablespoon butter	1¹/2 pounds fresh shrimp, peeled,
1¹/2 teaspoons curry powder	deveined and well drained
1¹/4 teaspoons salt	2 tablespoons lemon juice
1 tomato, chopped	1 cup sour cream
1 onion, chopped	3 or 4 avocados

Melt the butter in a skillet. Stir in the curry powder and salt. Add the tomato, onion and shrimp
and sauté until the shrimp are pink and cooked through. Add the lemon juice and mix well. Drain some
of the liquid if the mixture is thin. You may prepare to this point and chill until ready to complete the
preparation. Stir in the sour cream and cook until heated through, stirring occasionally. Spoon the
warm mixture into avocado halves.

Yield: 6 to 8 servings

SPICY MELON SALSA

*Lots of color and flavor make this salsa a must for any summer fiesta. Serve with
tortilla chips for a cool starter, or spoon over fish for a white-hot entrée.*

2¹/2 cups diced cantaloupe	1 jalapeño chile, seeded and
1 cup diced fresh or canned pineapple	finely chopped
1 red bell pepper, diced	2 tablespoons lime juice
2 scallions, thinly sliced	2 tablespoons mild olive oil
2 tablespoons chopped fresh cilantro	

Combine the cantaloupe, pineapple, bell pepper, scallions, cilantro, jalapeño, lime juice and olive
oil in a large bowl and toss gently. Chill, covered, until ready to serve.

Yield: 16 servings

PRALINE NUTS

Sour cream makes these pralines creamy and simply delicious.

1 cup sugar
1/2 cup sour cream

1/2 teaspoon vanilla extract
2 cups pecan halves

Cook the sugar and sour cream in a heavy 2-quart saucepan over medium heat to 252 degrees on a candy thermometer, soft-ball stage, stirring constantly. Remove from the heat and quickly stir in the vanilla and pecans. Pour onto waxed paper and cool. Break into pieces and store in an airtight container.

Yield: about 2 cups

CRUNCHY STUFFED OLIVES

Tampa's Pelagia Trattoria offers many varieties of olives, and this signature appetizer from Executive Chef Fabrizio Schenardi provides a way to savor their flavor apart from a cocktail.

1/2 cup plus 2 tablespoons
chopped onion
2 tablespoons chopped garlic
Olive oil (do not use virgin olive oil or extra-virgin olive oil)
1/2 pound each ground beef,
ground pork and ground veal
1/4 cup dry white wine
Salt and pepper to taste
2 tablespoons chopped fresh thyme

2 tablespoons grated lemon zest
1/2 cup (2 ounces) grated
Parmigiano-Reggiano cheese
1/8 teaspoon nutmeg
30 green Sicilian olives, pitted
1 1/2 cups all-purpose flour
5 eggs, beaten
2 cups bread crumbs
Vegetable oil
Lemon wedges

Sauté the onion and garlic in olive oil in a large skillet until softened. Add the beef, pork and veal and cook until brown and crumbly, stirring frequently. Stir in the wine. Cook until the wine evaporates, stirring occasionally. Season with salt and pepper. Stir in the thyme, lemon zest and cheese. Let stand until cool. Stuff the olives with the cooled mixture. Roll the stuffed olives in the flour. Dip in the eggs and roll in the bread crumbs. Fry the olives in 325-degree vegetable oil in a large deep skillet for 2 minutes. Serve with lemon wedges.

Yield: 8 to 10 servings

SPANISH MEATBALLS

These delicious little meatballs in their aromatic sauce are the quintessential tapas. Serve with toothpicks
for an authentic tapas experience or top pasta or rice for a hearty meal on a chilly day.

8 ounces ground beef	Salt and pepper to taste
4 spring onions or green onions, thinly sliced	1 tablespoon olive oil
	3 tomatoes, chopped
2 garlic cloves, finely chopped	2 tablespoons red wine
2 tablespoons finely grated manchego cheese	2 teaspoons chopped fresh rosemary
	1/8 teaspoon sugar
2 teaspoons fresh thyme	Fresh thyme sprigs

Combine the ground beef, spring onions, garlic, manchego cheese, thyme, salt and pepper in a
bowl and mix well. Shape the mixture firmly into 12 small balls. Cook the meatballs in the olive oil in
a large skillet over medium-high heat for 5 minutes or until evenly browned, turning frequently. Add the
tomatoes, wine, rosemary and sugar. Season with salt and pepper. Reduce the heat and cook, covered,
over low heat for 15 minutes or until the meatballs are cooked through and the sauce is of the desired
consistency. Serve hot, garnished with thyme sprigs.

Yield: 4 servings

PAN CON TOMATE

Pan con tomate, or tomato toast, is a simple yet delicious
dish that is a standard when serving tapas. Slice a large loaf of rustic
white bread into 1/2-inch slices and toast it. Cut several tomatoes in
half, and rub the cut sides of the tomatoes into one side
of each piece of toast. Discard the tomato peels. This is messy, but
that's part of the fun! Drizzle extra-virgin olive oil over the
tomato, and season with salt to taste.

BACON AND SWISS TARTS

*These savory treats always vanish off the plate and are great
for any breakfast or brunch.*

1 (10-count) can flaky biscuits	1/2 small onion, chopped
8 slices bacon, crisp-cooked	3 ounces Swiss cheese, shredded
and crumbled	1/2 cup mayonnaise
1 Roma tomato, seeded and chopped	1 teaspoon basil

Preheat the oven to 375 degrees. Cut each biscuit into thirds and press into greased miniature muffin cups. Combine the bacon, tomato, onion, Swiss cheese, mayonnaise and basil in a bowl and mix well. Spoon the mixture into the prepared muffin cups. Do not overfill. Bake for 10 to 12 minutes or until golden brown.

Yield: 30 servings

MELON MANCHEGO WRAPS

*This refreshing summer treat brings together savory prosciutto and
manchego cheese with sweet melons. Substitute the melon with sliced dates and
apples or other seasonal fruits of your choosing.*

8 dried pitted dates	16 cantaloupe slices
3 ounces manchego cheese,	8 slices prosciutto, cut into halves
cut into 16 (1/2-inch-thick) slices	lengthwise

Cut the dates into halves lengthwise. Place a date half and a slice of manchego cheese on each cantaloupe slice. Wrap with a slice of prosciutto, securing with wooden picks. You may substitute two Granny Smith apples for the cantaloupe, if desired. Slice the apples into 16 wedges and sprinkle with lemon juice to prevent them from turning brown.

Yield: 16 servings

OYSTERS PEDRO

This tasty variation on oysters Rockefeller includes puff pastry instead of oyster shells.
Simpler preparation and clean-up make it the perfect party dish.

8 ounces chopped fresh spinach
3 tablespoons butter
2 tablespoons minced onion
3 tablespoons bread crumbs
1 teaspoons salt
Tabasco sauce to taste
3 (6-count) packages puff pastry shells
1 pint fresh oysters
Grated Parmesan cheese

Preheat the oven to 400 degrees. Combine the spinach, butter, onion, bread crumbs, salt and Tabasco sauce in a 2-quart saucepan. Cook over medium heat until the mixture is of a paste consistency, stirring frequently. Arrange the pastry shells with the tops up on an ungreased baking sheet. Bake for 15 minutes.

Remove the tops from the pastry shells. Place one oyster in each pastry shell. Top with the spinach mixture. Bake for 5 minutes. Sprinkle with the Parmesan cheese. Bake for 2 minutes longer.

Yield: 18 servings

INVITATION IDEAS

Send out invitations with an option for guests to RSVP with the
name of their favorite drink. During the holidays, send invitations a
month in advance; otherwise, two weeks is sufficient.

CARAMELIZED ONION AND GORGONZOLA CROSTINI

This easy, elegant crowd-pleaser complements red wine beautifully.

Olive oil
1 baguette, thinly sliced
2 onions, thinly sliced
1 tablespoon brown sugar
1/8 teaspoon salt

2 tablespoons olive oil
1 (5- to 8-ounce) package crumbled
Gorgonzola cheese
1/2 cup walnuts, toasted

Brush olive oil on the baguette slices. Toast the baguette slices until golden brown. Cook the onions, brown sugar, salt and olive oil in a skillet over low heat until the onions are caramelized, stirring frequently. Preheat the oven to 375 degrees. Arrange the baguette slices on a baking sheet. Top each slice with a tablespoon of onions. Sprinkle evenly with the Gorgonzola cheese. Top with the walnuts. Bake for 10 minutes or until brown.

Yield: 6 or 7 servings

CRAB PIE

Topped with red and green this elegant hors d'oeuvre is especially nice during the holidays.

11 ounces cream cheese, softened
2 tablespoons mayonnaise
1 tablespoon Worcestershire sauce
1 tablespoon lemon juice
2 to 4 pieces bacon, crisp-cooked and
crumbled, or 1/2 (3-ounce) jar
bacon bits

Dash of garlic salt
1 small onion, finely chopped
1 (6-ounce) jar chili sauce, or
1 (8-ounce) jar cocktail sauce
1 (6-ounce) can crab meat, drained and
flaked
Finely chopped fresh parsley

Mix the cream cheese, mayonnaise, Worcestershire sauce, lemon juice, bacon, garlic salt and onion in a bowl. Spread the mixture in a shallow serving dish. Chill, covered, for 8 to 10 hours. Pour the chili sauce over the mixture. Sprinkle with the crab meat and parsley. Serve with crackers.

Yield: 6 to 8 servings

CRAB AND BRIE DIP WITH ARTICHOKES

A nice accompaniment to cocktails. Leek, tarragon, and dill weed
give this dip a unique flavor that will draw a crowd.

1 leek, white part only, finely chopped, washed and drained
1 sweet onion, finely chopped
2 tablespoons minced garlic
Vegetable oil
1/2 cup drained canned artichoke hearts, rinsed and chopped
1/2 cup finely chopped spinach
1/4 cup medium-dry white wine
2/3 cup heavy cream
1 pound Brie cheese, rind removed
3 tablespoons finely chopped fresh parsley

2 tablespoons finely chopped fresh dill weed
1 tablespoon finely chopped fresh tarragon
1 pound jumbo lump crab meat
2 tablespoons mayonnaise
2 tablespoons Dijon mustard
1 teaspoon Tabasco sauce, or 1/2 teaspoon cayenne pepper, or to taste
Salt and pepper to taste

Cook the leek, onion and garlic in oil in a skillet over medium heat until the vegetables are pale golden brown, stirring constantly. Add the artichoke hearts, spinach and wine. Cook for 2 to 4 minutes or until the mixture is simmering, stirring constantly. Stir in the cream and simmer for 1 minute. Slice the Brie cheese and add to the mixture. Cook until the cheese melts, stirring constantly. Remove from the heat and stir in the parsley, dill weed and tarragon.

Preheat the oven to 365 degrees. Combine the crab meat, mayonnaise, Dijon mustard, Tabasco sauce, salt and pepper in a bowl and mix well. Add to the cheese mixture and mix well. Spread evenly in a lightly greased shallow baking dish or 11-inch gratin dish. Bake for 15 to 20 minutes or until the top is golden brown. Serve with thin baguette slices or crackers.

Yield: 4 to 6 servings

CHUTNEY CHEESE SPREAD

An unusual cheese spread with a variety of colors, flavors, and textures.
You may prepare this ahead of time and chill until ready to serve.

8 ounces cream cheese, softened
2 cups (8 ounces) shredded
Cheddar cheese
1/4 cup sherry (optional)
1/2 teaspoon curry powder
1/2 to 1 (15-ounce) jar mango chutney

Finely chopped green onion tops
or shallots
2 to 4 pieces bacon, crisp-cooked and
crumbled, or 1/2 (3-ounce) jar
bacon bits

Combine the cream cheese, Cheddar cheese, sherry and curry powder in a bowl and mix well. Spread the mixture in a shallow serving dish. Top evenly with the chutney. Sprinkle with the green onions and then the bacon. Serve with wheat crackers.

Yield: 8 to 10 servings

SUN-DRIED TOMATO AND PESTO GOAT CHEESE

This is a delicious layered spread for any festive occasion.

8 ounces cream cheese, softened
1/2 cup (1 stick) butter, softened
2 ounces goat cheese, crumbled

1 (6-ounce) jar pesto
3/4 cup minced sun-dried tomatoes
Sprig of fresh basil

Combine the cream cheese and butter in a mixing bowl and beat until fluffy. Add the goat cheese and mix well. Spread half the cream cheese mixture in a shallow serving dish. Spread the pesto over the cream cheese layer. Spread the remaining cream cheese mixture over the pesto. Top with the sun-dried tomatoes. Garnish with a basil sprig and serve with crackers.

Yield: 4 to 6 servings

GOOD LUCK BEAN DIP

A delicious way to get your lucky serving of black-eyed peas on New Year's Day.

3 (15-ounce) cans black-eyed
peas, drained
5 to 8 jalapeño chiles from a jar,
seeded and chopped
1 teaspoon jalapeño chile liquid
from a jar
1/2 onion, chopped

1 (4-ounce) can chopped green
chiles, drained
1 garlic clove, minced
1/2 cup (1 stick) unsalted butter
8 ounces shredded sharp
Cheddar cheese

Mash a few of the black-eyed peas in a bowl with a fork. Add the remaining black-eyed peas, the jalapeños, jalapeño liquid, onion, green chiles and garlic and mix well. Combine the butter and Cheddar cheese in the top of a double boiler set over simmering water and heat until melted, stirring frequently. Add the black-eyed pea mixture and mix well. Cook until heated through. Serve warm with corn chips or tortilla chips. You may prepare the mixture in the microwave, if desired. Combine the butter and cheese in a microwave-safe bowl and cook on Medium, stirring every 30 seconds. Add the black-eyed pea mixture and cook until heated through, stirring every 30 seconds.

Yield: 6 to 8 servings

VIDALIA ONION DIP

This simple Southern dish merges sweet Vidalia onions with Parmesan and Swiss cheeses.

3 large Vidalia onions or other sweet
onions, cut into bite-size pieces
2 cups mayonnaise (do not use light)

2 cups (8 ounces) shredded Swiss cheese
2 drops hot sauce
Parmesan cheese to taste

Preheat the oven to 350 degrees. Combine the onions, mayonnaise, Swiss cheese and hot sauce in a bowl and mix well. Spoon into a shallow baking dish. Sprinkle with Parmesan cheese. Bake for 20 minutes or until the top is brown. Serve with crackers.

Yield: 8 servings

BROCCOLI ORANGE SALAD

Sweet raisins, crunchy pecans, and colorful oranges make the
perfect salad to complement a summertime barbecue.

4 cups fresh broccoli florets
(about 1¹/2 pounds)
1 small purple onion, very thinly sliced
and separated into rings
¹/2 cup raisins or dried cherries
¹/2 cup pecan pieces, toasted

³/4 cup mayonnaise or mayonnaise-type
salad dressing (may use reduced fat)
¹/4 cup sugar
1¹/2 tablespoons white vinegar
1 (11-ounce) can mandarin
oranges, drained

Place the broccoli in boiling water to cover in a saucepan and boil for 1 to 2 minutes. Plunge the broccoli in ice water immediately to stop the cooking process; drain. Combine the broccoli, onion, raisins and pecans in a bowl and toss gently. Combine the mayonnaise, sugar and vinegar in a small bowl and mix well. Add to the broccoli mixture and stir gently to coat. Add the mandarin oranges and stir gently. Chill, covered, for 3 hours or longer before serving.

Yield: 6 servings

SUMMERTIME MELON SALAD

This ambrosial fruit salad is ideal for any summertime celebration.

¹/2 (6-ounce) can frozen lemonade
concentrate, thawed
¹/4 cup orange marmalade
2 tablespoons Triple Sec
¹/2 cup fresh strawberry halves

2 cups assorted melon balls, such as
cantaloupe, honeydew and
seedless watermelon
1 small pineapple, cubed
Fresh mint sprigs

Combine the lemonade concentrate, marmalade and liqueur in a bowl and mix well. Combine the strawberries, melon balls and pineapple in a large bowl and toss gently. Pour the lemonade mixture over the fruit and stir gently. Chill, covered, for 2 hours or longer. Garnish with mint sprigs.

Yield: 6 to 8 servings

CREAMY FROZEN CRANBERRY SALADS

These pink frozen salads are served individually as a part of many family Thanksgiving and Christmas dinners. They would also be perfect for a spring or summer luncheon.

8 ounces cream cheese, softened	1/2 cup chopped pecans or pistachios
2 tablespoons sour cream	1 cup heavy whipping cream
1 (16-ounce) can whole cranberry sauce	1/2 cup sifted confectioners' sugar
1 (8-ounce) can crushed pineapple, drained	1 teaspoon vanilla extract
	Fresh whole cranberries
	Fresh mint sprigs

Beat the cream cheese and sour cream in a bowl until blended. Add the cranberry sauce, pineapple and pecans and mix well. Beat the whipping cream in a mixing bowl until foamy. Add the confectioners' sugar gradually, beating constantly until soft peaks form. Stir in the vanilla. Fold the whipped cream into the fruit mixture. Spoon into ten paper-lined muffin cups and freeze. Remove the frozen salads from the paper cups and place on lettuce-lined plates. Garnish with fresh cranberries and mint sprigs. You may freeze in sealable plastic freezer bags, if desired. The salads will keep in the freezer for up to 2 months.

Yield: 10 servings

STRAWBERRY SPINACH SALAD

The combination of this dressing and the spinach, strawberries, and almonds makes a fantastic salad.

1/2 cup chopped onion	2 tablespoons sesame seeds
1/2 cup sugar	1 tablespoon poppy seeds
1/4 cup vegetable oil	1 pound spinach, rinsed and torn
1/4 cup balsamic vinegar	1 pint strawberries, sliced
1/4 teaspoon Worcestershire sauce	1/2 cup slivered almonds, toasted

Combine the onion, sugar, oil, balsamic vinegar, Worcestershire sauce, sesame seeds and poppy seeds in a blender and process until smooth. Chill until ready to serve. Place the spinach on salad plates. Top with the strawberries and almonds. Drizzle with the dressing.

Yield: 4 to 6 servings

GRAPEFRUIT AND BLUE CHEESE SALAD WITH TOASTED WALNUTS

A refreshing salad for spring or summer.

3/4 cup dry red wine	1 garlic clove
1/2 cup port	3/4 cup canola oil
1/4 cup sugar	6 cups Bibb lettuce, torn
1/4 cup white balsamic vinegar	1 large pink grapefruit, sectioned
1/4 teaspoon kosher salt	2 to 3 ounces blue cheese, crumbled
1 small shallot, minced	1/2 cup chopped toasted walnuts

Cook the red wine, port and sugar in a nonstick skillet over medium-high heat for 20 minutes or until reduced to 1/4 cup, stirring frequently. Let cool slightly. Process the wine mixture, balsamic vinegar, salt, shallot and garlic in a blender until smooth. Add the canola oil in a fine stream, processing constantly until blended. Chill until ready to serve. Place the lettuce in a large salad bowl. Top with the grapefruit. Sprinkle the blue cheese and walnuts over the grapefruit. Drizzle with the dressing and toss gently to coat.

Yield: 4 servings

SENSATIONAL SALADS

For salads that call for nuts, meat, fruit, and/or cheese, follow these guidelines: For every 1 cup of greens, use 1/2 cup of nuts, meat, fruit, or cheese (use 1/4 cup for stronger cheeses such as Gorgonzola or goat cheese). When using a combination of nuts, meat, fruit, or cheese, decrease the amount to 1/4 cup each per 1 cup of greens. In recipes calling for heads or bunches of lettuce, a head of romaine usually yields 3 to 4 cups. Many recipes call for more dressing than needed. Add the dressing slowly, toss, and use your best judgment on quantity.

DINNER PARTY SALAD

*An old standard for dinner parties and gatherings, the shallots in the
dressing offer a mild, pleasing flavor.*

2 tablespoons heavy whipping cream
1 tablespoon red wine vinegar
2 teaspoons Dijon mustard
1/2 teaspoon salt
Freshly ground pepper to taste
1 shallot, finely chopped
1 garlic clove, crushed
2 tablespoons olive oil
1 head iceberg lettuce, torn into bite-size pieces
1/4 cup chopped walnuts, toasted
2 tablespoons chopped fresh parsley

Combine the cream, red wine vinegar, Dijon mustard, salt, pepper, shallot and garlic in a bowl and mix well. Whisk in the olive oil. Add the lettuce and toss to coat. Add the walnuts and parsley and toss gently. Serve immediately.

Yield: 4 to 6 servings

GINGERED CHINESE CHICKEN PASTA SALAD

Asian influences and a variety of textures make this
colorful pasta salad anything but typical.

1/2 cup rice vinegar
1/4 cup creamy peanut butter
1/4 cup toasted sesame oil
2 tablespoons soy sauce
2 tablespoons honey
2 tablespoons chopped fresh ginger
Salt and pepper to taste
2 cups chopped cooked chicken

16 ounces farfalle, cooked
al dente and drained
1 cup shredded carrots
1/2 cup julienned snow peas
1/4 cup chopped fresh cilantro
1/4 cup thinly sliced green onions
1/2 cup peanuts

Combine the rice vinegar, peanut butter, sesame oil, soy sauce, honey, ginger, salt and pepper in a blender and process until smooth and blended.

Combine the chicken, pasta, carrots, snow peas, cilantro and green onions in a large bowl. Add the dressing and toss gently to coat. Sprinkle with the peanuts. You may add 2 tablespoons chipotle chile purée, Tabasco sauce or your favorite hot sauce to make the salad spicier, if desired.

Yield: 6 to 8 servings

LOW-CARB OPTION

Substitute half a head of cabbage for the pasta to
make a great low-carb meal. The sauce doubles as a dressing
when poured over bow tie pasta with chicken or as a sauce
for grilled chicken satay skewers.

SEARED TUNA NIÇOISE

*A wonderful variation on the traditional French dish using
sushi-grade tuna. Serve with a warm baguette.*

RED WINE AND DIJON DRESSING
3 tablespoons red wine vinegar
1 tablespoon fresh lemon juice
2 teaspoons Dijon mustard
1 teaspoon anchovy paste
2 tablespoons minced fresh tarragon
1 garlic clove, minced
1/3 cup extra-virgin olive oil
Kosher salt to taste
Fresh ground pepper to taste

SALAD
6 red new potatoes, cut into halves
1 pound haricots verts
   (French green beans)
1 pound sushi-grade tuna steak
1 tablespoon olive oil
Kosher salt to taste
Fresh ground pepper to taste
3 tomatoes, cut into quarters
3 cups mixed salad greens
1/2 cup niçoise olives or kalamata olives
3 eggs, hard-cooked and cut into
   halves lengthwise

For the dressing, combine the red wine vinegar, lemon juice, Dijon mustard, anchovy paste, tarragon and garlic in a large glass bowl and mix well. Add the olive oil gradually, whisking constantly until blended. Season with salt and pepper.

For the salad, boil the potatoes in water to cover in a saucepan until fork tender; drain. Bring a large pot of water to a rolling boil. Add the green beans and boil for 3 minutes. Plunge the beans in ice water immediately to stop the cooking process. Heat a large, heavy skillet over medium-high heat. Brush the tuna on all sides with the olive oil. Season with salt and pepper. Place the tuna in the hot skillet and cook for 2 minutes on each side. Place the tuna on a cutting board and cut into 1/2-inch slices.

For the assembly, add the potatoes to the dressing and toss gently to coat. Remove the potatoes with a slotted spoon and arrange on a serving platter. Repeat the procedure with the beans, tomatoes, salad greens and olives. Arrange the eggs around the edge of the platter. Place the tuna on the top of the salad. Serve any remaining dressing on the side.

Yield: 6 servings

CAVA COCKTAIL

This cocktail is the perfect drink to accompany our Holiday Tapas
menu or any holiday open house.

2 cups unsweetened pineapple juice
1 cup brandy
1 cup Triple Sec
1/2 cup Chambord
4 cups ginger ale, chilled
2 (750-milliliter) bottles cava, chilled

Combine the pineapple juice, brandy and liqueurs in a large bowl. Chill, covered, for 4 hours or longer. Pour the mixture into a punch bowl. Add the ginger ale and cava and mix well. You may substitute extra-dry Champagne for the cava.

Yield: 29 (4-ounce) servings

CHAMPAGNE ALTERNATIVE

A Spanish sparkling wine, cava is a delicious and well-priced
alternative to French Champagne. It is usually served
at weddings, birthdays, and Christmas and New Year's celebrations.
Cava may be found in fine wine specialty shops. Well-known
producers include Freixenet and Juve i Camps.

POMEGRANATE MARGARITA

*Here is the margarita recipe you've been looking
for—the pomegranate juice takes it from blah to bling!*

2 cups pomegranate juice	2 cups margarita mix
1 cup tequila	1 cup orange juice
1 cup orange liqueur, such as Triple Sec	

Combine the pomegranate juice, tequila, liqueur, margarita mix and orange juice in a large pitcher and stir until blended. Pour over ice into glasses. You may substitute cranberry juice for the pomegranate juice, if desired.

Yield: 4 to 6 servings

KEY LIME PIE MARTINI

*A great after-dinner drink instead of a dessert, this can be served
during any occasion to add Florida flair.*

1 lime, cut into wedges	4 ounces (1/2 cup) lime juice
Crushed graham crackers	4 ounces (1/2 cup) half-and-half
6 ounces (3/4 cup) Licor 43®	

Squeeze the juice from one of the lime wedges onto a saucer. Place the graham cracker crumbs on a saucer. Dip the rim of a martini glass in the lime juice and then dip in the graham cracker crumbs. Combine the Licor 43, lime juice, half-and-half and ice in a cocktail shaker and shake well. Pour through a strainer into the prepared glass. Garnish with a lime wedge.

Yield: 4 servings

SIPPIN' SANGRIA

Serve this red sangria over ice with pieces of fresh fruit.
Sip on a glass while tasting tapas.

1 (1.5-liter) bottle Frontera Concha
y Toro Cabernet Sauvignon/Merlot
1 cup vodka
2 cups orange juice
1 cup sugar

1/4 teaspoon ground cinnamon
Orange slices
Apple slices
3 (12-ounce) cans lemon-lime soda

Combine the wine, vodka, orange juice, sugar, cinnamon, orange slices and apple slices in a large container and stir until the sugar is dissolved. Chill in the refrigerator until ready to serve. Add the soda just before serving.

Yield: 10 to 12 servings

ZIPPY STRAWBERRY ICED TEA

Strawberries are abundant in central Florida during the late winter and early spring.
The bubbly strawberry and lemon flavors give this alcohol-free drink a real zip.

2 cups strawberries, cut into halves
1/2 cup sugar
6 cups water
2 (single-serving-size) tea bags

1 (12-ounce) can frozen lemonade
concentrate, thawed
1 (1-liter) bottle club soda, chilled

Purée the strawberries in a blender or food processor. Combine the strawberry purée and sugar in a bowl and stir until the sugar is dissolved. Chill, covered, until ready to use. Bring the water to a rapid boil in a saucepan. Remove from the heat and add the tea bags. Let steep for 5 minutes. Remove and discard the tea bags. Let the tea cool to room temperature. Combine the strawberry purée and lemonade concentrate in a large pitcher or punch bowl and mix well. Add the tea and club soda and mix well. Serve over ice.

Yield: 12 servings

PEPPERMINT EVE EGGNOG

Christmas Eve eggnog with a twist—Santa's sure to love it!

1 pint peppermint ice cream, softened
2 cups eggnog
1 (28-ounce) bottle club soda, chilled
Few drops red food coloring

1 cup heavy whipping cream, whipped
1/3 cup crushed peppermint candy
16 peppermint sticks

Spoon the ice cream into a punch bowl. Add the eggnog and club soda and mix well. Stir in the food coloring. Top with the whipped cream. Spoon the eggnog into glasses. Sprinkle with the crushed peppermint candy and serve with a peppermint stick.

Yield: 16 servings

HOT MULLED CIDER

Warm your guests on a cold day with this classic winter treat.

1 (64-ounce) bottle apple cider or
apple juice
1 (12-ounce) can frozen orange juice
concentrate, thawed
1/2 cup lemon juice

1 teaspoon whole cloves
1 teaspoon allspice
4 cinnamon sticks
4 orange slices
Additional cinnamon sticks

Combine the apple cider, orange juice concentrate and lemon juice in a large saucepan. Wrap the cloves, allspice and four cinnamon sticks in cheesecloth and tie with kitchen twine. Add to the cider mixture. Bring the mixture to a boil and boil for 5 minutes. Reduce the heat and add the orange slices. Simmer for 30 minutes, stirring occasionally. Serve warm garnished with a cinnamon stick.

Yield: 8 to 10 servings

COMPLEMENTS

CURRIED PUMPKIN CRAB BISQUE

*A savory blend of traditional fall spices combined with the mouthwatering
sweetness of succulent crab. This is a soup you will never forget.*

1 small onion, finely chopped
4 garlic cloves, minced
2 tablespoons curry powder
2 teaspoons ground ginger or
2 tablespoons grated fresh ginger
1 teaspoon ground nutmeg
1/2 teaspoon Tabasco sauce
1/2 cup (1 stick) butter, melted
1 tablespoon cornstarch

1 (16-ounce) can pumpkin purée
4 cups chicken broth
2 cups heavy cream
2 cups fresh lump back-fin
    crab meat, flaked
Salt and pepper to taste
Cognac (optional)
Fresh or dried parsley

Cook the onion, garlic, curry powder, ginger, nutmeg and Tabasco sauce in the butter in a stockpot
until the onion is tender, stirring frequently. Stir in the cornstarch and cook until thickened. Add the
pumpkin and broth and bring the mixture to a boil. Reduce the heat and simmer for 15 minutes, stirring
occasionally. Stir in the cream and crab meat. Cook until thickened and bubbly, stirring constantly.
Season with salt and pepper. Ladle into soup bowls. Pour a splash of cognac over each serving. Sprinkle
with parsley.

Yield: 8 to 10 servings

OUT OF YOUR GOURD

*For gourmet presentation at your autumn dinner or
Thanksgiving feast, serve Curried Pumpkin Crab Bisque in colorful
gourds, such as acorn squash. Slice a bit off the rounded base
of the gourd to help it lay flat, and line the inside bottom with foil to
ensure the soup doesn't leak. Garnish with small pieces
of crab, a dash of cognac, and fresh parsley.*

ITALIAN WEDDING SOUP

Chef Paolo Tini of Caffé Paradiso shared this signature soup from his award-winning restaurant. This soup is popular at Italian weddings and is now served for all sorts of occasions. For a heartier soup, add Spanish Meatballs (page 31).

2 quarts chicken broth
1/2 pound spinach, rinsed and trimmed
2 tablespoons Parmesan cheese
2 eggs, beaten
Additional Parmesan cheese

Bring the broth to a boil in a stockpot. Stir in the spinach, 2 tablespoons Parmesan cheese and the eggs. Reduce the heat and cook until the eggs rise to the top, stirring occasionally. Reduce the heat to low and cook for 1 minute longer. Ladle into soup bowls and sprinkle with additional Parmesan cheese.

Yield: 4 to 6 servings

STORING OPEN WINE

From the moment you uncork a bottle of red or white wine,
oxidation begins, gradually causing the flavor to fade. To preserve
wine for a day or two, replace the cork and store it in the
refrigerator. Chilling slows the oxidation process. For longer storage,
invest in a wine vacuum, which removes the oxygen from the bottle.
Return red wine to room temperature before serving.

SHERRIED MUSHROOM SOUP

Sherry gives a rich, finishing touch to this creamy soup. Serve as an elegant
first course or with a substantial salad to make a meal.

1/2 pound assorted mushrooms, such as portobello,
porcini or shiitake, sliced
1/3 cup finely chopped onion
3 tablespoons butter
2 tablespoons all-purpose flour
1 (10-ounce) can beef broth
2 cups half-and-half
1/4 cup dry sherry
1 teaspoon dried basil, or 1 tablespoon chopped fresh basil
1/2 teaspoon dried tarragon, or
1 1/2 teaspoons chopped fresh tarragon
Salt and pepper to taste

Sauté the mushrooms and onion in 2 tablespoons of the butter in a 2-quart saucepan over medium heat until the mushrooms and onion are tender. Remove the mushroom mixture to a bowl. Melt the remaining 1 tablespoon butter in the saucepan. Add the flour and cook for 1 minute, stirring constantly.

Add the broth gradually, stirring constantly. Add the half-and-half gradually, stirring constantly. Cook until thickened, stirring frequently. Add the mushroom mixture, sherry, basil, tarragon, salt and pepper and mix well. Reduce the heat and simmer for 10 to 15 minutes or until heated through. Ladle into soup bowls.

Yield: 6 servings

MARINATED ASPARAGUS WITH CHERRY TOMATOES

*This quick and easy side dish is perfect during the holidays when
you want a delicious, attractive vegetable in a flash.*

2 pounds asparagus, steamed	2 teaspoons orange juice
15 cherry tomatoes, cut into halves	1/8 teaspoon salt
1/2 garlic clove, minced	1/8 teaspoon pepper
1 cup olive oil	6 green onions, chopped
1/2 cup balsamic vinegar	1 green bell pepper, chopped
1/4 cup sugar	1/4 cup chopped pimento

Place the asparagus and tomatoes in a large sealable plastic bag. Combine the garlic, olive oil, balsamic vinegar, sugar, orange juice, salt and pepper in a bowl and whisk until blended. Pour over the asparagus and tomatoes. Add the green onions, bell pepper and pimento. Chill in the refrigerator for 8 to 10 hours.

Yield: 6 to 8 servings

ACORN SQUASH BOWLS

The perfect harvest vegetable is a baked acorn squash.

Just cut acorn squash in half and scoop out the seeds. Cut the stem

from the bottom and place stem side down in a baking dish with one

inch of water. Add butter, salt, and pepper to taste along with spices

to complement your entrée. For a sweeter version, try cinnamon

and nutmeg. More savory options would be rosemary or thyme with

garlic. Bake, loosely covered with foil, at 350 degrees for

20 minutes or until tender.

NOUVEAU HOLIDAY GREEN BEANS

The best thing that has happened to the original Green Bean Casserole. Sun-dried tomatoes, green beans, and white feta cheese create a festive look.

BASIL VINAIGRETTE
4 garlic cloves, finely minced
1/2 cup extra-virgin olive oil
2 tablespoons balsamic vinegar
1 tablespoon chopped fresh basil
1 teaspoon salt
1/2 teaspoon pepper

GREEN BEANS
2 to 3 pounds fresh green beans, trimmed
1/2 pound bacon
2 onions, finely chopped
1 (4-ounce) package sun-dried tomatoes, chopped
4 ounces feta cheese, crumbled
1/2 cup chopped almonds

For the vinaigrette, combine the garlic, olive oil, balsamic vinegar, basil, salt and pepper in a large bowl and whisk until blended.

For the green beans, combine the green beans with boiling water to cover in a saucepan. Boil just until the green beans are tender; do not overcook. Plunge the green beans in ice water immediately to stop the cooking process; drain. Cook the bacon in a skillet until brown and crisp. Remove with a slotted spoon to a paper towel-lined plate, reserving the bacon drippings. Let the bacon stand until cool and then crumble. Cook the onions in the reserved bacon drippings until tender, stirring frequently. Add the green beans, bacon, onions, sun-dried tomatoes, feta cheese and almonds to the vinaigrette and toss gently.

Yield: 4 to 6 servings

KITCHEN SCENTSATIONS

Simmer cut oranges, lemons, and cinnamon sticks in water

on your stove to add a seasonal aroma to your kitchen and humidify

the dry, winter air. If you are using your fireplace, add a few

orange peels to the fire for a fresh scent.

GLAZED CARROTS

Amaretto brings a wonderful flavor to classic buttered carrots.

1/4 cup (1/2 stick) butter
1/2 cup packed brown sugar
Grated zest and juice of 1 orange
2 (10-ounce) packages matchstick
    carrots, or 1 1/2 pounds
    carrots, julienned

1 tablespoon amaretto, or 1 teaspoon
    almond flavoring
Salt to taste
1/2 cup slivered almonds (optional)

Melt the butter in a saucepan over medium heat. Add the brown sugar and cook until the brown sugar is dissolved and the mixture is bubbly, stirring constantly. Stir in the orange zest and juice. Add the carrots and reduce the heat to low. Cook for 10 minutes or until the carrots are tender and glazed, stirring frequently. Add the amaretto and cook until heated through. Season with salt and sprinkle with almonds.

Yield: 6 to 8 servings

HERB-ROASTED FINGERLING POTATOES WITH CAVIAR

Caviar adds a touch of luxury to these delicate potatoes.

1 pound unpeeled fingerling potatoes,
    cut into halves lengthwise
1 tablespoon olive oil
1 teaspoon minced fresh parsley
1 teaspoon minced fresh rosemary

1 teaspoon minced fresh thyme
Salt and pepper to taste
1/4 cup chilled crème fraîche or
    sour cream
Caviar

Preheat the oven to 400 degrees. Toss the potatoes, olive oil, parsley, rosemary and thyme in a bowl. Season with salt and pepper. Arrange the potatoes, cut side down, on a large rimmed baking sheet. Roast for 35 minutes or until the potatoes are brown, crisp and cooked through. Cool on the baking sheet for 10 minutes. Arrange the potatoes on a serving plate and serve with dollops of crème fraîche and caviar.

Yield: 4 servings

POTATO LEEK GRATIN

*Leeks and a dash of cayenne pepper make this potato gratin
extraordinary. Serve with a simple roast chicken and a bottle of Beaujolais,
and you'll feel like you're eating in a Parisian café.*

3 pounds large baking potatoes, peeled
and thinly sliced
2 teaspoons salt
1/4 cup (1/2 stick) butter
2 cups chopped leeks (1 to 2 leeks)
1/4 cup flour
3 cups milk, warmed

1 teaspoon salt
1/8 teaspoon white pepper
1/8 teaspoon cayenne pepper
2 cups (8 ounces) shredded Cheddar
cheese blend
1/2 cup crushed Club crackers

Combine the potatoes and 2 teaspoons salt with cold water to cover in a large saucepan. Bring to a boil and boil for 8 minutes; drain. Rinse the potatoes and pat dry with paper towels.

Preheat the oven to 375 degrees. Melt the butter in a saucepan over medium heat. Add the leeks and cook for 6 to 8 minutes or until softened. Mash the leeks with a fork. Sprinkle the flour over the leeks and whisk until of a paste consistency. Add half the milk, whisking constantly until smooth. Repeat with the remaining milk. Add 1 teaspoon salt, the white pepper and cayenne pepper and mix well. Bring to a boil, whisking frequently. Remove from the heat and stir in 1 1/2 cups of the cheese.

Layer half the potato slices in a 9×13-inch baking dish sprayed with nonstick cooking spray. Spoon half the leak mixture over the potatoes. Layer with the remaining potatoes and leek mixture. Sprinkle with the remaining 1/2 cup cheese. Bake for 20 minutes. Sprinkle with the cracker crumbs. Bake for 10 minutes or until the cracker crumbs are light brown. Let stand for 10 minutes before serving.

Yield: 8 servings

Sweet Potato Soufflé with Pecan Streusel

A soufflé is a delightfully different way to include sweet potatoes in your holiday menu.

1 cup packed brown sugar
1/3 cup all-purpose flour
1 cup chopped pecans
1/3 stick butter
3 cups mashed cooked sweet potatoes
1 cup half-and-half

1/3 stick butter, melted
2 eggs
3/4 cup packed brown sugar
1 teaspoon vanilla extract
1/2 teaspoon salt

Preheat the oven to 325 degrees. Combine 1 cup brown sugar, the flour and pecans in a small bowl and mix well. Cut in 1/3 stick butter until crumbly.

Combine the sweet potatoes, half-and-half, 1/3 stick melted butter, the eggs, 3/4 cup brown sugar, the vanilla and salt in a large bowl and mix well. Spoon into a greased baking dish. Sprinkle with the pecan topping. Bake for 1 hour.

Yield: 12 servings

Romantic Interludes

Plan a special dinner to suit your style as a couple. If you're the expressive type who loves to get sentimental, go for it. Write a poem, letter, or card that says how much your beloved means to you. Or maybe you are subtler in expressing your feelings. Keep it light-hearted with a humorous twist. Many couples fall somewhere in between, so why not balance the two? Find something you have in common and make that the focus.

SWEET POTATOES WITH RUM AND WATER CHESTNUTS

Water chestnuts and pineapple are interesting additions to this sweet potato casserole.

1 (9-ounce) can crushed pineapple
2 Granny Smith apples, finely chopped
1 (7-ounce) can water chestnuts, drained
2 (16-ounce) cans sweet
potatoes, drained and mashed

3 tablespoons butter
1/3 cup sugar
3 tablespoons rum
1/2 tablespoon ground cinnamon
1/2 tablespoon ground ginger

Preheat the oven to 350 degrees. Drain the pineapple, reserving the juice. Mix the pineapple, apples, water chestnuts and sweet potatoes in a bowl. Combine the butter, sugar, rum, reserved pineapple juice, cinnamon and ginger in a saucepan and cook over medium-low heat until the mixture is of a syrup consistency, stirring frequently. Pour over the sweet potato mixture. Spoon into a buttered 9×13-inch baking dish. Bake for 45 minutes.

Yield: 9 to 12 servings

STUFFED TOMATOES

An easy dinner party side dish with elegant presentation.

4 or 5 tomatoes
1 (5-ounce) jar Old English
cheese spread
2 tablespoons butter, softened
1/4 cup chopped green onions

1/4 cup bread crumbs
3 slices bacon, crisp-cooked
and crumbled
Salt and pepper to taste

Preheat the oven to 350 degrees. Slice the stem end off each tomato. Scoop the pulp out and remove the seeds. Chop and drain the pulp. Place the tomatoes, cut side down, on paper towels to drain. Combine the cheese spread and butter in a bowl and mix well. Add the tomato pulp, green onions, bread crumbs, bacon, salt and pepper and mix well. Spoon into the tomato halves and arrange the tomatoes on a baking sheet. Bake for 25 to 30 minutes or until the tops are brown.

Yield: 4 or 5 servings

TOASTED PARMESAN ZUCCHINI

Beautiful presentation makes this the perfect cocktail party hors d'oeuvre or side dish.

4 zucchini, cut into halves lengthwise
1 egg, beaten
1/3 cup Italian bread crumbs
1/3 cup grated Parmesan cheese

1 garlic clove, minced
1/2 teaspoon salt
1/2 teaspoon pepper
Shaved Parmesan cheeese

Preheat the oven the 350 degrees. Place the zucchini a large saucepan of boiling water. Boil for 8 to 10 minutes or just until softened. Do not overcook. Remove the zucchini from the water and let cool. Scoop the pulp into a bowl, reserving the shells. Add the egg, bread crumbs, 1/3 cup Parmesan cheese, garlic, salt and pepper to the pulp and mix well. Spoon the mixture into the reserved shells. Arrange the filled shells on a baking sheet. Sprinkle with Parmesan cheese shavings. Bake for 10 to 12 minutes or until golden brown on top. Let stand for 2 minutes before serving.

Yield: 4 to 8 servings

PINEAPPLE CASSEROLE

Simple and sweet. Is it a side dish or a dessert? You decide!

1 1/2 cups sugar
3 eggs
1/2 cup milk
1/2 cup (1 stick) butter, softened

4 cups packed white bread cubes
1 (20-ounce) can crushed pineapple,
    drained

Preheat the oven to 350 degrees. Combine the sugar, eggs and milk in a bowl and mix well. Stir in the butter, bread cubes and pineapple. Spoon into a greased 7×9-inch baking dish. Bake on the middle rack of the oven for 30 to 40 minutes or until golden brown, crispy on top and cooked through. Let stand for 10 minutes before serving.

Yield: 6 servings

FRUITED HOLIDAY COMPOTE

This recipe is our answer to how to prepare the ubiquitous and ever-popular cranberry for a traditional Thanksgiving meal.

1 pound fresh cranberries	1 teaspoon grated lime zest
1/4 cup finely chopped peeled apples	1 teaspoon grated orange zest
1/4 cup finely chopped peeled pears	1/4 cup orange juice
1 cup sugar	

Combine all the ingredients in a heavy saucepan. Bring to a boil, skimming the foam from the top. Boil for just under 1 minute. Reduce the heat to medium-low and simmer for 10 minutes or until the cranberries pop, stirring occasionally. Pour into a serving bowl and cool to room temperature.

Yield: 10 servings

BRAZILIAN NEW YEAR'S LENTILS

This recipe was submitted by Vanessa Souza, executive chef of Dinner Done.
Born in Brazil, Chef Souza serves this hearty dish to her family on New Year's Day.
In both Brazil and Italy, lentils are said to bring good luck.

6 cups water	$1^{1}/_{2}$ teaspoons vegetable base, such as
1 cup lentils	Better than Bouillon
3 tablespoons butter	2 large yellow onions, thinly sliced
2 cups basmati rice	1/2 teaspoon sugar
1 teaspoon salt	Chopped fresh parsley

Bring 2 cups of the water to a boil in a small saucepan. Add the lentils and cook for 10 minutes, stirring occasionally; drain. Heat 2 tablespoons of the butter in a large saucepan over medium-high heat. Stir in the rice and salt. Add the remaining 4 cups water, the vegetable base and lentils and bring to a boil. Stir gently and reduce the heat to low. Simmer, tightly covered, for 20 minutes or until the rice and lentils are tender. Melt the remaining 1 tablespoon butter in a sauté pan. Add the onions and sugar and sauté until the onions are golden brown. Spoon over the rice and garnish with parsley.

Yield: 6 servings

HOPPIN' JOHN

Another fabulous recipe from Dinner Done owner and food enthusiast Dan Nasser.
This is his version of the Southern dish traditionally served on New Year's Day. It is said to bring luck
and prosperity, with black-eyed peas symbolizing coins and greens symbolizing paper currency.

1 1/2 cups finely chopped onion
1 cup finely chopped green bell pepper
3/4 teaspoon salt
2 tablespoons canola oil
5 cups water
1 tablespoon vegetable base,
   such as Better than Bouillon
1 (12-ounce) package black-eyed peas,
   rinsed and sorted

1 carrot, finely chopped (about 1 cup)
2 cups finely chopped pork, beef or
   turkey kielbasa
1 (32-ounce) package white rice
1 (16-ounce) package fresh collard
   greens, rinsed and trimmed
1 to 2 teaspoons salt, or to taste
Red wine vinegar or cider vinegar
   to taste

Sauté the onion, bell pepper and 3/4 teaspoon salt in the canola oil in a saucepan over medium-high heat until the onion is light brown. Stir in the next 5 ingredients. Reduce the heat to low. Simmer, tightly covered, for 2 hours or until the black-eyed peas are tender. Prepare the rice using the package directions. Serve the black-eyed peas over the rice. Combine the collard greens with water to cover in a stockpot. Add 1 to 2 teaspoons salt and simmer for 1 hour or until the greens are tender, stirring occasionally. Serve with red wine vinegar.

Yield: 6 servings

HOPPIN' JOHN HISTORY

There are several theories about where the name "Hoppin' John"
originated. Some say children had to hop around the table before
eating it. Others say a man named John came a hoppin' when his
wife made it. Perhaps the most convincing explanation is that
Americans mispronounced a French-Caribbean dish called "pois a
pigeon" or pigeon peas (black-eyed peas) and made it their own.

APPLE WALNUT DRESSING

A Thanksgiving staple, this distinctive dressing combines the autumnal flavors of Italian sausage, mushrooms, sage, walnuts, Granny Smith apples, and more.

1 pound Italian sausage, casings removed
2 cups finely chopped onions
8 garlic cloves, minced
4 ribs celery, finely chopped
1 cup sliced mushrooms
1 (14-ounce) package stuffing mix with sage and onions

1 cup chopped walnuts
8 sprigs fresh Italian parsley, stems removed and leaves finely chopped
4 sprigs fresh sage, stems removed and leaves finely chopped
1 cup chicken stock, or to taste
1 Granny Smith apple, peeled and finely chopped

Preheat the oven to 350 degrees. Brown the sausage in a skillet, stirring until crumbly. Remove the sausage to a bowl using a slotted spoon. Drain and discard all except 1 tablespoon of the pan drippings. Add the onions, garlic, celery and mushrooms to the reserved drippings and cook until the vegetables are softened, stirring frequently.

Add the sausage and mix well. Spoon the mixture into a large baking dish. Add the stuffing mix, walnuts, parsley, sage and chicken stock and mix well. Add the apples and mix gently. Bake for 30 minutes or until brown on top.

Yield: 6 to 8 servings

DRESSING OR STUFFING?

Ever wondered what the difference is between these two items that accompany a holiday turkey? The two are basically the same, but stuffing is often placed in the cavity of the turkey, while dressing is served on the side. In the Southeast, people usually call it dressing, while in the Northeastern United States, it's referred to as stuffing.

SAVORY CHEESE BREAD

This is the perfect bread to accompany a variety of dishes.

2 envelopes yeast
3 tablespoons sugar
2 cups warm water (approximately 110 degrees)
1 cup (4 ounces) shredded sharp Cheddar cheese
1 tablespoon butter, softened
1 tablespoon salt
4 1/2 cups all-purpose flour

Dissolve the yeast and sugar in the water in a small bowl. Combine the cheese, butter and salt in a mixing bowl and mix well. Add the yeast mixture and mix well. Add the flour gradually, beating constantly. Place the dough in a round 2-quart baking dish sprayed with nonstick cooking spray. Let rise in a warm, draft-free place for 30 to 45 minutes. Push the dough down with a spatula. Let rise for 30 to 45 minutes or until the dough has risen to just above the side of the dish. Preheat the oven to 350 degrees. Bake for 45 minutes or until the bread sounds hollow when tapped on the top of the loaf. Let stand until cool.

Yield: 8 to 10 servings

BREAD VARIATIONS

For variations on this bread recipe, consider adding

1 1/2 cups grated Parmesan cheese and 2 tablespoons chopped

fresh thyme or rosemary.

GREEN CHILE AND CHEDDAR CORN BREAD

*Classic corn bread spiced up a bit with cumin and green chiles. Try it at
a Fourth of July barbecue or a New Year's day brunch.*

1 cup yellow cornmeal
1/2 teaspoon salt
1/2 teaspoon baking soda
1/4 teaspoon cayenne pepper
1/4 teaspoon ground cumin
3/4 cup sour cream
1/3 cup butter, melted

1 (8-ounce) can cream-style corn
2 eggs, beaten
1 cup (4 ounces) shredded Cheddar
   cheese or Mexican cheese blend
1 (4-ounce) can chopped green
   chiles, drained

Preheat the oven to 375 degrees. Grease an 8-inch ovenproof skillet and place over medium heat. Combine the cornmeal, salt, baking soda, cayenne pepper and cumin in a bowl and mix well. Add the sour cream, butter, corn and eggs and stir until blended. Spoon half the mixture into the hot skillet. Sprinkle evenly with the cheese and chiles. Top with the remaining batter. Bake for 30 to 40 minutes or until golden brown and a wooden pick inserted in the center comes out clean.

Yield: 8 servings

MONSTER MIX

Make your own Halloween trail mix as a portable treat

for your little monsters. Mix one part eye of newt

(M&M chocolate candies), one part rat toenails (sunflower

seeds or roasted pumpkin seeds), one part spider eggs

(raisins), and one part vampire fangs (candy corn). Feel free

to get creative with additional ingredients. Put it in cute

Halloween cups, and it's ready to go for trick-or-treaters.

CHOCOLATE SWIRL BANANA BREAD

A delicious treat for children and adults alike! Could double as dessert with
whipped cream or as breakfast served with fresh fruit and coffee.

3/4 cup chocolate chips
1/4 cup (1/2 stick) butter, softened
1 cup sugar
3 overripe bananas, chopped
2 eggs
1/3 cup sour cream
21/4 cups all-purpose flour
3/4 teaspoon baking soda
1/2 teaspoon salt

Preheat the oven to 350 degrees. Microwave the chocolate chips in a microwave-safe bowl for
1 minute or until melted, stirring every 30 seconds. Cream the butter and sugar on medium speed in a
mixing bowl. Add the bananas, a few pieces at a time, beating constantly. Add the eggs and sour cream
and beat until blended. Add the flour, baking soda and salt gradually, beating constantly on low speed.

Add half the batter to the melted chocolate and stir until smooth. Drop alternating large spoonfuls
of the banana batter and the chocolate batter into a greased 4×8-inch loaf pan. Swirl the two batters
using a knife. Bake for 1 hour and 15 minutes. Cool in the pan for 15 minutes. Remove to a wire rack
to cool completely.

Yield: 8 servings

FOR YOUR LITTLE PUMPKINS

For a great party favor at your child's Halloween gathering, wrap

a handful of small chocolates or other favorite candies in orange

crepe paper. Shape the crepe paper into a ball and tape it together

with green crepe paper at the top to look like a pumpkin.

EGGNOG TEA BREAD

If you enjoy the nutmeg and vanilla flavors of eggnog and the sweetness of cake, you'll love this festive holiday treat.

3 cups all-purpose flour
1¹/2 teaspoons baking powder
1/2 teaspoon nutmeg
1/2 teaspoon salt
1 cup (2 sticks) unsalted butter, softened
1³/4 cups granulated sugar

4 eggs, at room temperature
1 teaspoon vanilla extract
1 cup eggnog, at room temperature
1 cup sifted confectioners' sugar
2 to 3 tablespoons eggnog
1/8 teaspoon nutmeg

Preheat the oven to 325 degrees. Whisk together the flour, baking powder, 1/2 teaspoon nutmeg and the salt in a bowl. Cream the butter and granulated sugar in a mixing bowl. Add the eggs one at a time, beating constantly and stopping to scrape down the side of the bowl occasionally. Add the vanilla and mix well. Add the flour mixture alternately with 1 cup eggnog, beating until the mixture is smooth.

Spray a bundt pan or two large loaf pans with nonstick cooking spray. Sprinkle with flour and shake out the excess. Pour the batter into the prepared pan. Bake for 55 minutes for the bundt pan or for 30 to 35 minutes for the loaf pans or until a wooden pick inserted near the center comes out clean. Cool in the pan for 10 minutes. Invert onto a serving platter to cool completely.

Combine the confectioners' sugar, 2 to 3 tablespoons eggnog and 1/8 teaspoon nutmeg in a small bowl and mix well. Pour over the cooled bread. For a more spirited glaze, you may substitute 1 tablespoon spiced rum for 1 tablespoon of the eggnog.

Yield: 10 to 12 servings

Peanut Butter Pumpkin Bread

This versatile recipe can be served at breakfast or dessert. Miniature loaves make excellent additions to Christmas baskets for neighbors.

3$^1/2$ cups all-purpose flour	2 cups canned pumpkin
3 cups sugar	$^2/3$ cup water
1 teaspoon baking soda	$^1/2$ cup vegetable oil
$^1/2$ teaspoon salt	4 eggs
1$^1/2$ teaspoons ground cinnamon	1 (10-ounce) package peanut
1 teaspoon ground ginger	butter chips

Preheat the oven to 350 degrees. Combine the flour, sugar, baking soda, salt, cinnamon and ginger in a medium bowl. Combine the pumpkin, water, oil and eggs in a mixing bowl and beat until blended. Add the flour mixture gradually, beating constantly until blended. Stir in the peanut butter chips. Pour into three greased and floured 5×9-inch loaf pans or seven greased and floured miniature loaf pans. Bake for 55 to 70 minutes for the standard loaf pans or for 45 to 65 minutes for the miniature loaf pans or until a wooden pick inserted in the center comes out clean. Let cool in the pans for 10 minutes. Remove wire racks to cool completely.

Yield: 3 large loaves or 7 miniature loaves

Magic Reindeer Food

As your children anticipate the arrival of Santa and his team of reindeer, help them make a special treat for Dasher, Dancer, and company. Mix equal parts of sunflower seeds, oatmeal, and sugar. Add a small amount of silver glitter. Divide it into sandwich bags and attach a reindeer-shaped label with the rhyme: "Sprinkle this on your lawn today, to help Santa's reindeer find the way." Share the Magic Reindeer Food with your friends, family, and neighbors.

OVERNIGHT FRENCH TOAST

*Prepare this breakfast/brunch entrée the night before and pop it in the oven when
you awaken. The divine aroma will lure family members to the kitchen.*

1 loaf French bread, cut into 3/4-inch slices	1/3 cup maple syrup
8 ounces cream cheese, softened	12 eggs
1 1/2 cups milk	Maple syrup
	Whipped cream
	Fresh fruit

Arrange a layer of bread in a 9×13-inch baking pan sprayed with nonstick cooking spray.
Spread half the cream cheese over the bread. Arrange the remaining bread on the cream cheese layer.
Spread the remaining cream cheese on the bread. Whisk together the milk and syrup in a bowl. Add
the eggs one at a time, whisking constantly until blended. Pour over the prepared layers. Cover the
dish with plastic wrap. Weight the plastic wrap with two boxes confectioners' sugar or cake mix so
that the plastic is touching the layers. Chill overnight in the refrigerator.

Preheat the oven to 350 degrees. Bake, uncovered, for 30 to 40 minutes or until the eggs are set.
Let stand for 10 minutes loosely covered with aluminum foil. Serve with warm maple syrup, whipped
cream and fresh fruit. You may spread your favorite flavor preserves over each layer of cream cheese
for extra flavor, if desired.

Yield: 8 servings

THE NIGHT BEFORE CHRISTMAS

*For many families, Christmas morning is a time for
opening gifts, attending church, or just relaxing together. To make
the morning a bit more relaxing, try putting together dishes
the day or night before that can be easily heated or baked without
much time spent in the kitchen. Be sure to set the
table on Christmas Eve, too.*

CRANBERRY WALNUT SCONES WITH HONEY ORANGE CREAM

Traditionally served with tea or coffee, these scones are great for a holiday breakfast or on a tea tray. They also freeze beautifully; just reheat in the oven for 5 to 10 minutes or until heated through.

SCONES
3 cups all-purpose flour
1/2 cup sugar
1 tablespoon baking powder
1/2 teaspoon baking soda
1/2 teaspoon salt
3/4 cup (11/2 sticks) butter, cut into small pieces
1 cup fresh cranberries, finely chopped, or 1/2 cup dried cranberries
1/2 cup chopped walnuts
11/2 teaspoons grated orange zest

1/2 to 1 cup buttermilk
1 egg, beaten
1 teaspoon water
1/2 tablespoon sugar
1/4 teaspoon ground cinnamon
1/8 teaspoon ground allspice

HONEY ORANGE CREAM
8 ounces cream cheese, softened
2 tablespoons honey
1 tablespoon grated orange zest

For the scones, preheat the oven to 400 degrees. Combine the flour, 1/2 cup sugar, the baking powder, baking soda and salt in a large bowl. Cut in the butter with a pastry blender or rub in with your fingers until the mixture resembles coarse crumbs. Stir in the cranberries, walnuts and orange zest. Add the buttermilk and stir just until the mixture is moistened and forms a dough.

Shape the dough into a ball and place on a floured work surface. Pat the dough 3/4-inch thick. Cut into rounds using a 21/2-inch cutter. Arrange the dough rounds 11/2-inches apart on a greased baking sheet. Whisk together the egg and water in a small bowl. Brush over the tops of the dough rounds. Combine 1/2 tablespoon sugar, the cinnamon and allspice in a bowl. Sprinkle over the dough rounds. Place the baking sheet on the lower rack of the oven and bake for 14 to 16 minutes or until the tops are light brown. Serve warm with honey orange cream.

For the cream, combine the cream cheese, honey and orange zest in a mixing bowl and beat until light and fluffy. Spread over the warm scones. You may prepare the cream up to two days in advance. Store, covered, in the refrigerator.

Yield: 12 servings

Centerpieces

MUSTARD-ROASTED CORNISH HENS

Rosemary, mustard, and garlic add autumnal flavors to this delicious French entrée.

2 to 4 Cornish hens
Olive oil
Salt and pepper to taste
1/2 cup dry white wine
1/2 cup chicken broth
2 tablespoons Dijon mustard
1 1/2 teaspoons dry mustard
2 tablespoons minced fresh rosemary
1 tablespoon chopped garlic
1 1/2 tablespoons butter, melted
2 tablespoons butter, softened

Preheat the oven to 450 degrees. Remove the backbones from the hens using a sharp knife or poultry scissors. Lay each hen flat with the skin side up. Rub the hens with olive oil and season with salt and pepper. Combine the wine and broth in a roasting pan. Place the hens, skin side up, in the roasting pan. Roast for 10 minutes.

Mix the Dijon mustard, dry mustard, rosemary and garlic in a bowl. Add 1 1/2 tablespoons melted butter and mix well. Spread the mixture over the skin of the hens. Roast for 25 to 35 minutes or until the hens are golden brown and the juices run clear when the thighs are pierced, basting occasionally with the pan juices.

Remove the hens from the roasting pan and let stand for 15 minutes. Pour the pan juices into a skillet. Cook over medium heat until reduced and of a sauce consistency, stirring frequently. Remove from the heat and whisk in 2 tablespoons softened butter. Drizzle the sauce over the warm hens. You may also roast the whole hens by tying the legs together using kitchen twine. Roast as directed above.

Yield: 2 to 4 servings

ALMOND-CRUSTED CHICKEN IN STRAWBERRY SAUCE

An elegant dish that is easy to make and bursting with flavor.

CHICKEN
1 tablespoon olive oil
4 boneless skinless chicken breasts
1/2 teaspoon salt
1/4 teaspoon pepper
1/3 cup finely chopped
   unblanched almonds

STRAWBERRY SAUCE
1/4 cup minced shallots or green onions
1/3 cup chicken broth

1/3 cup strawberry preserves
3 tablespoons balsamic vinegar
1 tablespoon minced fresh rosemary,
   or 1 teaspoon dried rosemary,
   crumbled

ASSEMBLY
1 (10-ounce) bag fresh spinach,
   steamed
Finely chopped fresh parsley

For the chicken, heat the olive oil in a large nonstick skillet sprayed with cooking spray over medium-high heat. Sprinkle the chicken with the salt and pepper. Coat with the almonds. Place the chicken in the skillet and cook for 4 minutes on each side, turning once. Remove to a platter with a slotted spoon. Keep the chicken warm.

For the sauce, add the green onions to the skillet and sauté over low heat for 1 minute. Add the chicken broth, strawberry preserves, balsamic vinegar and rosemary. Simmer for 2 to 3 minutes or until the mixture thickens slightly, stirring frequently.

For the assembly, place the spinach on a heated serving platter. Top with the chicken. Pour the sauce over the chicken. Sprinkle with parsley.

Yield: 4 servings

THAI CHICKEN WITH COCONUT RICE

Serve this delicious chicken dish with coconut rice for a truly authentic Thai meal.

8 boneless skinless chicken thighs (about 2 pounds)
3/4 cup hot salsa
1/4 cup peanut butter
2 tablespoons lime juice
1 tablespoon soy sauce

1 teaspoon grated fresh ginger
3 cups rice
1 1/4 cups coconut milk
1 1/4 cups water
1/4 cup chopped peanuts
2 tablespoons chopped fresh cilantro

Place the first 6 ingredients in a slow cooker. Cook on Low for 8 to 9 hours or until the chicken is cooked through. Prepare the rice using the package directions, using the coconut milk and water. Spoon the rice onto plates. Spoon the chicken over the rice. Sprinkle with the peanuts and cilantro.

Yield: 4 to 6 servings

TOASTED BRIE CHICKEN TEA SANDWICHES

These sandwiches are dainty additions to your tea tray.

2 pounds boneless skinless chicken breasts, cubed
2 cups chicken broth
1 cup mayonnaise
1 cup red grapes, sliced
3 ribs celery, finely chopped

2 teaspoons Italian herbs
2 teaspoons pepper
1 teaspoon onion powder
6 to 12 croissants
2 (8-ounce) wheels Brie cheese, rind removed and cheese sliced

Preheat the oven to 375 degrees. Combine the chicken and broth in a roasting pan. Roast for 12 to 18 minutes or until cooked through. Do not allow the chicken to brown. Drain and discard the broth. Place the chicken in a large bowl and let stand until cool. Mix the mayonnaise, grapes, celery, Italian herbs, pepper and onion powder in a bowl. Stir in the chicken. Cut each croissant into halves crosswise and cut each half into halves horizontally. Toast the croissants. Place a slice of brie on half of the croissant pieces. Top with the chicken mixture and the remaining croissant pieces.

Yield: 12 to 24 sandwiches

SESAME-CRUSTED CHICKEN SALAD TEA SANDWICHES

An Asian twist on traditional chicken salad.

1 unpeeled onion, cut into halves
6 black peppercorns
2 sprigs fresh thyme
1 bay leaf
3¹/2 pounds chicken breasts
¹/2 cup plus 2 tablespoons mayonnaise
1 tablespoon (or more) dark sesame oil
¹/4 cup chopped fresh cilantro
2 tablespoons chopped chives

3 scallions, white and light green parts
    thinly sliced crosswise
Kosher salt to taste
Freshly ground black pepper, to taste
24 thin slices white bread,
    crusts trimmed
¹/2 cup plus 2 tablespoons unsalted
    butter, softened
¹/4 cup sesame seeds, toasted

Place the onion, peppercorns, thyme and bay leaf in a stock pot. Add the chicken and cold water to cover. Cover and bring to a simmer. Remove the cover and simmer for 1 hour, stirring occasionally. Drain the chicken and reserve the stock for future use. Let the chicken cool. Remove and discard the chicken skin and bones. Shred and finely chop the chicken. Refrigerate, covered, until chilled.

Combine the mayonnaise and sesame oil in a small bowl and stir until blended. Add to the chicken and mix well. Add the cilantro, chives and scallions and mix well. Season with salt and pepper. Chill, covered, until ready to serve.

Spread the butter evenly on one side of each bread slice. Spread the chicken salad evenly over half the bread slices. Top with the remaining bread slices. Cut each sandwich diagonally into halves. Butter the two short sides of each sandwich. Spread the sesame seeds over the buttered sides. Arrange the sandwiches buttered side up on a serving platter.

Yield: 24 tea sandwiches

GRILLED CHICKEN PANINI

*This Italian sandwich is made on a round, crusty roll with a
crispy outside and a coarse texture inside.*

PESTO SAUCE
1 cup firmly packed fresh basil
1/2 cup fresh parsley
1/4 cup toasted pine nuts
2 or 3 garlic cloves
1 teaspoon salt, or to taste
1 teaspoon pepper, or to taste
1/4 cup olive oil
1/2 cup (2 ounces) grated Parmesan
cheese or Romano cheese

PANINI
4 boneless skinless chicken breasts
Salt and pepper to taste
Olive oil
8 slices sourdough bread
4 slices provolone cheese
1 (7-ounce) jar roasted red bell peppers
8 fresh basil leaves

For the pesto, combine the basil, parsley, pine nuts, garlic, salt and pepper in a food processor and
process until finely chopped. Add the olive oil gradually, processing constantly until blended. Add the
Parmesan cheese and pulse to combine.

For the panini, combine the chicken and pesto sauce in a bowl and marinate, covered, in the
refrigerator for 3 hours. Remove the chicken from the pesto and discard the pesto. Season the chicken
with salt and pepper. Grill the chicken over hot coals until cooked through, turning once. Spread olive
oil over the bread slices and grill the bread until golden brown on both sides. Place a chicken breast
on four of the bread slices. Top each with a slice of provolone cheese, some of the roasted red peppers
and two basil leaves. Top with the remaining bread slices. Cut into halves and serve immediately.

Yield: 4 sandwiches

SMOKED TURKEY

Cherry or hickory wood chips
1 (15- to 20-pound) turkey
1 bottle red wine
2 oranges, sliced
4 red apples, sliced
5 sprigs fresh rosemary

5 sprigs fresh thyme
Olive oil
Kosher salt and pepper to taste
1 sweet onion, cut into quarters
5 ribs celery, cut into 3-inch pieces

Combine the wood chips with warm water to cover in a bowl and let soak for 2 hours or longer. Let the turkey stand at room temperature for 30 minutes. Combine the wine, oranges, 2 apples, 2 sprigs rosemary and 2 sprigs thyme in the smoker water pan. Add enough water to almost fill the pan. Place the water pan in the smoker and light the charcoal. Brush olive oil on the inside and outside of the turkey. Season the inside and outside of the turkey with salt and pepper. Place the onion, celery, remaining apples, rosemary and thyme in the cavity of the turkey. Add the wood chips to the hot coals.

Place the turkey on the top grill rack of the smoker and close the lid tightly. Do not remove the cover. Smoke for 6 to 8 hours or until a meat thermometer inserted in the turkey thigh reads 180 degrees. Maintain the heat at 200 to 225 degrees and add additional wood chips as needed to maintain the smoke for the first 3 to 4 hours. Remove the turkey and let stand for 10 minutes before carving.

Yield: 10 to 12 servings

TANGY BBQ SAUCE

This tangy sauce, perfect for chicken, pork, or ribs, has been in
a Junior League of Tampa member's family for generations. Simmer
4 cups apple cider vinegar, 2 cups corn oil, 1 cup yellow mustard,
1 cup water, 1/2 cup ketchup, 5 tablespoons Worcestershire sauce,
1/4 cup salt, 1 tablespoon Tabasco sauce, 1 tablespoon onion
salt, 5 teaspoons red pepper and 1 teaspoon black pepper in a saucepan
for 10 minutes, stirring constantly. Yield: 1/2 gallon sauce.

STACKED TURKEY WITH CRANBERRY CREAM CHEESE

*Great with Thanksgiving leftovers or any time of the year,
these sandwiches are layered with sweet and sour cucumbers, cranberry
cream cheese, and cashews. Serve with a riesling.*

CUCUMBERS
1 cup thinly sliced cucumber
1/2 cup thinly sliced onion
1/2 cup white wine vinegar
1 tablespoon sugar
Pinch of salt

CRANBERRY CREAM CHEESE
4 ounces cream cheese, softened
(may use reduced fat)
1/4 cup dried cranberries, minced
Juice of 1/2 lemon

1/4 teaspoon minced fresh rosemary
or thyme
Salt and pepper to taste

ASSEMBLY
8 slices whole wheat bread or other
hearty bread
1/4 cup chopped cashews
12 ounces roasted or fried turkey, sliced
(may use deli turkey)
Salt and pepper to taste

For the cucumbers, combine the cucumber, onion, white wine vinegar, sugar and salt in a bowl and stir gently.

For the cream cheese, combine the cream cheese, cranberries, lemon juice, rosemary, salt and pepper in a bowl and mix well.

For the assembly, spread one side of each bread slice with 1 tablespoon of the cranberry cream cheese. Sprinkle evenly with the cashews. Top half of the bread slices with the cucumbers. Arrange the turkey over the cucumbers. Season with salt and pepper and top with the remaining bread slices. Cut each sandwich into halves.

Yield: 4 sandwiches

TURKEY CHIPOTLE CHILI

1 pound mild turkey sausage
1 onion, chopped
5 garlic cloves, chopped
1 tablespoon kosher salt
2 teaspoons chili powder
1 teaspoon dried oregano
3 tablespoons extra-virgin olive oil
1 tablespoon tomato paste
1 chipotle chile en adobo,
    coarsely chopped

1 tablespoon adobo sauce
12 ounces Mexican lager-style beer
1 (14-ounce) can peeled whole tomatoes
1 (15-ounce) can kidney beans, drained
    and rinsed
2 ounces milk chocolate or semisweet
    chocolate
Chopped scallions, cilantro, avocado
    slices, sour cream and shredded
    Monterey Jack cheese

Remove the casings from the turkey sausage. Cook the onion, garlic, salt, chili powder and oregano in the olive oil in a large skillet over medium-high heat for 3 minutes or until fragrant, stirring frequently. Stir in the tomato paste, chipotle chile and adobo sauce and cook for 1 minute. Add the turkey sausage and cook for 3 to 4 minutes or until brown and crumbly, stirring occasionally with a wooden spoon. Add the beer and reduce the heat. Simmer for 8 minutes or until the liquid is reduced by half.

Crush the undrained tomatoes into the skillet using your hands. Add the beans and chocolate and mix well. Increase the heat and bring to a boil. Boil, uncovered, for 10 minutes or until thickened, stirring occasionally. Spoon into serving bowls and garnish with scallions, cilantro, avocado, a dollop of sour cream and Monterey Jack cheese. Serve with tortilla chips.

Yield: 4 servings

ADOBO PASTE

In Mexican cooking, adobo can be a paste for rubbing

on meats, a marinade for all kinds of foods, or a sauce;

it usually contains chiles and vinegar.

ROASTED BEEF TENDERLOIN WITH BRANDY CREAM SAUCE

This classic entrée is great for a crowd or a couple. Cut the meat quantity in half when serving for two. It's sure to make your romantic evening or dinner party unforgettable.

BEEF TENDERLOIN
1 garlic clove, minced
1/2 cup olive oil
1/4 cup (1/2 stick) unsalted butter
1/4 cup cooking sherry
2 to 4 tablespoons red wine vinegar
Dash of Worcestershire sauce
2 tablespoons salt (do not use kosher)
1 tablespoon finely crushed black pepper
1 (2-pound) short loin beef tenderloin

BRANDY CREAM SAUCE
1 cup dry white wine
1/2 cup brandy
2 1/2 cups veal stock or low-sodium beef stock
8 to 10 black peppercorns, coarsely crushed
1 tablespoon red currant jelly
1/2 cup heavy cream

For the beef, preheat the oven to 350 degrees. Combine the garlic, olive oil, butter, sherry, red wine vinegar, Worcestershire sauce, salt and pepper in a shallow bowl and mix well. Roll the tenderloin in the mixture to coat thoroughly and place the tenderloin in a baking dish. Bake for 25 to 35 minutes for rare or for 30 to 45 minutes for medium rare. Slice the tenderloin at a 45-degree angle. Serve with the brandy cream sauce.

For the sauce, heat a heavy-bottom skillet over high heat. Cook the wine and brandy in the skillet until reduced by two-thirds, stirring frequently. Stir in the veal stock and peppercorns. Cook until the sauce is of a syrup consistency, stirring frequently. Pour the sauce through a fine sieve or cheesecloth and return to the skillet, discarding the solids. Add the jelly and cream and cook until heated through. Do not boil.

Yield: 6 to 8 servings

SKIRT STEAK WITH CHIMICHURRI

Chimichurri sauce comes from Latin America, with variations
according to region. It's delicious served with grilled steak. Make it as spicy
as your taste buds can handle!

2 large tomatoes, seeded and chopped	1½ teaspoons dried oregano
2 garlic cloves, minced	½ teaspoon salt
⅔ cup olive oil	2 (1-pound) skirt steaks
3 tablespoons red wine vinegar	Salt and pepper to taste
1½ teaspoons red pepper flakes	

Combine the tomatoes, garlic, olive oil, red wine vinegar, red pepper flakes, oregano and ½ teaspoon salt in a bowl and mix well. Let stand for several hours to allow the flavors to blend. Season the steaks with salt and pepper. Grill over hot coals to the desired degree of doneness. Cut the steaks at a slight angle across the grain and place on a serving platter. Spoon the sauce over the steaks.

Yield: 4 to 6 servings

CULTURAL INFLUENCES TAKE THE CAKE

Tampa cuisine is blessed with many wonderful ethnic influences,

such as Cuban, Latin, Spanish, and more. Many of us

share holiday traditions that reflect our heritage, like Guava Rum

Cheesecake (page 98), a Christmas staple for one Junior

League of Tampa family. Flavor your holiday feast with your

own family recipes to make it more personal.

BOURSIN-STUFFED BURGERS WITH GARLIC AÏOLI

*A burger with melted garlic cheese, sun-dried tomatoes, and
caramelized onions is sure to make mouths water.*

GARLIC AÏOLI
1 jumbo egg
Juice of 1 lemon
1 tablespoon Dijon mustard
3 garlic cloves
1 cup vegetable oil

HAMBURGERS
1 sweet onion, chopped
Olive oil

2 pounds ground beef
Garlic salt to taste
Pepper to taste
1 (4- to 5-ounce) package boursin
   cheese
1/4 cup finely chopped sun-dried
   tomatoes
4 sandwich buns

For the aïoli, combine the egg, lemon juice, Dijon mustard and garlic in a blender and process until blended. Add the oil gradually, processing constantly until the mixture is thickened and of a mayonnaise consistency. Spoon into a bowl and chill, covered, until ready to serve. If you are concerned about using raw eggs, use eggs pasteurized in their shells, which are sold at some specialty food stores, or use an equivalent amount of pasteurized egg substitute.

For the hamburgers, cook the onion in olive oil in a skillet over medium heat until caramelized, stirring frequently. Combine the onion and ground beef in a bowl. Season with garlic salt and pepper and mix well using your hands. Combine the boursin and sun-dried tomatoes in a small bowl and mix well.

Shape the ground beef mixture into four patties, reserving some of the ground beef mixture. Make a well in the center of each patty and fill with the boursin mixture. Cover the filled wells with the reserved ground beef mixture, pressing the edges to seal. Grill the patties over hot coals to the desired degree of doneness. Brush the cut sides of the sandwich buns with olive oil. Brown the sandwich buns in the skillet used to caramelize the onions. Place the hamburgers on the buns and serve with the aïoli and your favorite condiments.

Yield: 4 servings

SPINACH-STUFFED LEG OF LAMB

This succulent entrée will enhance your Easter dinner or most any holiday meal.

2 pounds fresh spinach, stemmed
1 tablespoon salt
1 cup chopped green onions
1/3 cup olive oil
1 egg, beaten
1/4 cup dry bread crumbs
1/4 teaspoon dried dill weed
1/4 teaspoon dried oregano
1/8 teaspoon pepper

1 (7-pound) leg of lamb, butterflied
1/4 cup olive oil
3 tablespoons lemon juice
2 garlic cloves, minced
2 teaspoons dried oregano
2 teaspoons salt
1/2 teaspoon pepper
4 ounces feta cheese, cubed
1/4 cup chopped fresh parsley

Julienne the spinach and sprinkle with 1 tablespoon salt. Place the spinach in a colander and let stand for 1 hour. Squeeze the spinach to remove the moisture. Sauté the green onions in 1/3 cup olive oil in a large heavy skillet over medium heat for 2 minutes. Remove from the heat and let cool slightly. Stir in the egg, bread crumbs, dill weed, 1/4 teaspoon oregano and 1/8 teaspoon pepper.

Preheat the oven to 400 degrees. Place the lamb skin side down on a work surface. Combine 1/4 cup olive oil, the lemon juice, garlic, 2 teaspoons oregano, 2 teaspoons salt and 1/2 teaspoon pepper in a bowl and stir until blended. Rub half the olive oil mixture over the lamb. Top with the feta cheese. Spread the spinach mixture evenly over the feta cheese layer. Fold one-third of the lamb over the filling. Fold one-third of the lamb from the opposite end over the filling and tie with kitchen twine. Place the lamb in a roasting pan and rub with the remaining olive oil mixture. Roast for 30 minutes. Reduce the oven temperature to 350 degrees. Roast for 2 hours, basting frequently with the pan juices. Remove and discard the kitchen twine. Place the lamb on a serving platter and garnish with the parsley.

Yield: 4 to 6 servings

PORK TENDERLOIN WITH APRICOTS, FENNEL AND SHALLOTS

This dish is a great wintertime crowd-pleaser, especially when served with our Potato Leek Gratin (page 56).

2 to 2 1/2 pounds pork tenderloin	1 fennel bulb, trimmed and
Kosher salt to taste	thinly sliced
Fresh ground pepper to taste	1/2 cup chicken stock
6 generous tablespoons grainy mustard	18 to 20 dried apricots
3/4 cup plain dry bread crumbs	3/4 cup chicken stock
3 tablespoons vegetable oil	1/2 cup cognac
2 tablespoons unsalted butter	3/4 cup chicken stock
1 tablespoon vegetable oil	1 tablespoon fresh thyme
6 shallots, cut into quarters	Fresh thyme sprigs

Preheat the oven to 400 degrees. Season the pork with salt and pepper. Rub the mustard over the pork and coat with the bread crumbs. Heat 3 tablespoons oil in a heavy roasting pan over medium-high heat. Add the pork and cook until brown on all sides. Remove the pork from the pan. Add the butter and 1 tablespoon oil to the pan. Add the shallots and fennel and sauté for 5 to 6 minutes or until the shallots are tender. Add 1/2 cup chicken stock and cook for 2 minutes or until the liquid evaporates, stirring frequently.

Return the pork to the pan. Add the apricots, 3/4 cup chicken stock and the cognac. Roast for 25 to 30 minutes or until the pork reaches 160 degrees on a meat thermometer, basting the pork and turning the fruit and vegetables occasionally. Remove the pork to a cutting board. Add the remaining 3/4 cup chicken stock and the thyme to the roasting pan and deglaze the pan over medium-low heat. Cook until the sauce is thickened, stirring occasionally. Season with salt and pepper. Slice the pork and place on a serving platter. Arrange the fruit and vegetables around the pork and spoon the sauce over the top. Garnish with fresh thyme sprigs.

Yield: 6 to 8 servings

SWEET AND SPICY SUMMER RIBS

Get great-tasting oven-baked ribs, or use the outdoor grill for an old-fashioned smoky flavor. The sweet, spicy rub works well on meats, chicken, and fish.

DRY RUB
1 tablespoon each brown sugar,
granulated sugar, chili powder,
garlic powder, paprika and
kosher salt
2 teaspoons freshly ground pepper
2 teaspoons cumin
1½ teaspoons ancho chili powder
1 teaspoon coriander

RIBS
3 pounds baby back pork ribs
Kosher salt to taste
½ cup Dijon mustard

SAUCE
½ onion, cut into quarters
¼ cup water
1 cup ketchup
2 tablespoons each cider vinegar,
    Worcestershire sauce and molasses
3 tablespoons brown sugar
½ teaspoon hot red pepper sauce
½ teaspoon kosher salt
¼ teaspoon freshly ground pepper
2 garlic cloves, minced
1 teaspoon chili powder
2 tablespoons vegetable oil
1 chipotle chile, finely chopped

For the rub, combine all the ingredients in a bowl and mix well.

For the ribs, arrange the ribs on cooking racks and place the cooking racks on two large baking sheets. Sprinkle lightly with salt and brush with the Dijon mustard. Coat the ribs evenly with the dry rub. Let stand at room temperature for 1 hour. Preheat the oven to 250 degrees. Bake for 1½ to 2 hours or until the ribs are fork tender. Place each rack of ribs on a piece of aluminum foil. Fold the aluminum foil over the ribs to enclose. Place the foil packets in a brown paper bag and let stand for 1 hour or longer. Cut the ribs between the bones and arrange on a serving platter. Serve with the sauce. You may add 1 to 2 teaspoons liquid smoke to the Dijon mustard before rubbing on the ribs for a smoky flavor. You may substitute pork spareribs for the baby back ribs. Increase the cooking time by 2 to 3 hours.

For the sauce, process the onion and water in a food processor until of a syrup consistency. Pour the mixture through a sieve into a bowl, pressing to release the onion juice. Discard the solids. Stir the ketchup, cider vinegar, Worcestershire sauce, molasses, brown sugar, hot sauce, salt and pepper into the onion mixture. Cook the garlic and chili powder in the oil in a sauté pan over medium-low heat for 1 to 2 minutes or until fragrant, stirring frequently. Increase the heat and add the ketchup mixture and chipotle chile. Bring to a boil, stirring frequently. Reduce the heat to low and simmer for 30 minutes or until thickened, stirring occasionally. Let stand until cool.

Yield: 4 to 6 servings

BACON AND LEEK QUICHE

This delicious brunch quiche may also be served as individual miniature quiches.

1 (9-inch) pie pastry	1/4 teaspoon salt
1 tablespoon Dijon mustard	1/8 teaspoon pepper
1/2 pound bacon (about 8 pieces), chopped	3 eggs
	1 1/2 cups milk
2 cups chopped leeks (white and some green parts)	1 1/2 cups (6 ounces) shredded Gruyère cheese

Preheat the oven to 375 degrees. Fit the pie pastry in a 9-inch pie pan leaving some overhang on the side. Prick the bottom of the pastry several times with a fork. Line the pastry with aluminum foil and fill with pie weights, rice or beans. Bake for 20 minutes or just until the edge begins to brown. Remove the pie weights and foil. Decrease the oven temperature to 325 degrees. Spread the mustard over the baked crust.

Cook the bacon in a skillet over low heat just until it begins to brown. Add the leeks, salt and pepper and cook for 8 minutes or until the leeks are tender and the bacon is crisp, stirring frequently; drain. Combine the eggs and milk in a bowl and beat until blended. Add the leek mixture and cheese and mix well. Pour into the crust. Bake for 25 to 30 minutes or until the center is set. Let stand for 10 minutes before serving.

Yield: 6 to 8 servings

A GREEN CHRISTMAS

As an alternative to flowers, adorn your holiday table with festive

greenery and natural colors. Clip fir tree branches, holly

berries and leaves, or even magnolia branches, and arrange on a

rectangular silver or pewter platter. Add colorful fresh fruits

such as pears, apples, and grapes for interest.

SAUTÉED ISLAND GROUPER

Grouper, a fish native to Florida and the Caribbean, is perfectly paired with a banana nut rum sauce in this island-inspired recipe.

GROUPER	BANANA NUT RUM SAUCE
1 tablespoon butter	1 banana
2 (4-ounce) grouper fillets	2 tablespoons unsalted butter
Flour for dredging	2 teaspoons brown sugar
Salt and pepper to taste	2 tablespoons rum
Milk for coating	2 teaspoons water
	1/8 teaspoon cinnamon, or to taste
	2 tablespoons chopped pecans, toasted

For the grouper, melt the butter in a sauté pan. Combine flour, salt and pepper in a shallow dish. Dip the grouper in milk. Dredge in the flour mixture. Cook in the butter for 4 minutes or until golden brown. Do not lift the grouper from the pan during the cooking process. Turn the grouper and cook for 4 to 6 minutes or until golden brown on the outside and opaque in the center. Keep warm in the oven or tent loosely with foil. Do not cover tightly as this will steam the fish and cause the coating to become soggy.

For the sauce, cut the banana into halves lengthwise. Cut each half into halves crosswise. Melt the butter in a skillet over medium-high heat. Add the banana, cut side down. Cook for 1 minute. Remove the pan from the heat. Sprinkle the banana with the brown sugar. Pour in the rum slowly. Return the pan to the heat. Add the water and cinnamon and cook for 1 to 2 minutes or until the sauce thickens, shaking the pan gently. Be careful not to break up the banana. Spoon the banana mixture over the grouper and sprinkle with the pecans. Serve immediately.

Yield: 2 servings

SNAPPER ON FAVA BEAN PURÉE WITH FIG MARSALA REDUCTION

Submitted by Chef Jeannie Pierola, Chef and partner at SideBern's Restaurant and Executive Chef and Culinary Director at Bern's Steakhouse

FAVA BEAN PURÉE AND FIG MARSALA REDUCTION

3 cups shelled fava beans
1/4 cup extra-virgin olive oil
1 teaspoon fresh thyme leaves
Kosher salt and cracked black pepper to taste
1 cup marsala
1/2 cup dried mission figs
Juice and zest of 1 orange
2 bay leaves
2 tablespoons unsalted butter

SNAPPER

6 (6-ounce) snapper fillets
Kosher salt and cracked black pepper, to taste
1/4 cup extra-virgin olive oil
3 tablespoons unsalted butter
1/4 pound prosciutto, cut into strips
1 cup wild mushrooms
1 tablespoon minced shallot
1 teaspoon minced garlic
1 bag pea shoots
Extra-virgin olive oil
Butter

For the fava beans, boil the beans with 6 cups salted water in a saucepan until tender; drain. Purée the beans, olive oil, thyme, salt and pepper in a food processor. Keep warm until ready to serve.

For the reduction, boil the wine, figs, orange juice, orange zest and bay leaves in heavy saucepan until reduced by one third, stirring frequently. Remove the bay leaves. Process the reduction in a blender until smooth. Stir in the butter and season with salt and pepper.

For the snapper, preheat the oven to 325 degrees. Season the snapper with salt and pepper. Heat a large sauté pan over medium-high heat. Add half the olive oil and half the butter. Place a snapper fillet in the pan and sauté until golden brown. Turn the snapper gently and cook until golden brown. Place on an ovenproof platter and keep warm in the oven. The snapper will continue to cook in the oven; do not overcook. Repeat with the remaining snapper. Heat a sauté pan over medium-high heat. Add the remaining olive oil and butter. Add the prosciutto and sauté for 1 to 2 minutes. Add the mushrooms and sauté for 2 minutes. Add the shallots and then the garlic. Season with salt and pepper. Place the pea shoots in a large stainless steel bowl. Place olive oil and butter in a sauté pan over medium heat and heat just until the butter begins to foam. Pour the mixture over the pea shoots and toss gently. Season with salt and pepper. Place 3 to 4 ounces fava bean purée off-center on each of six heated dinner plates. Drizzle with the reduction sauce. Place the snapper on the plates and top with the mushroom mixture and the pea shoots. Drizzle with olive oil.

Yield: 6 servings

SEAFOOD PAELLA

*This is Spain's most famous rice dish. It makes for a spectacular presentation
and will have your guests thinking you spent hours in the kitchen.*

8 ounces monkfish or other dense
white fish, skinned and cut into
1-inch pieces
4 ounces baby squid, body cut into
rings and tentacles left whole
2 tablespoons olive oil
1 yellow onion, chopped
3 garlic cloves, finely chopped
1 red bell pepper, cut into 1-inch pieces
2 tablespoons olive oil
4 tomatoes, peeled, seeded and
finely chopped
1 1/4 cups short grain Valencian rice,
such as Alcazaba or Bomba, or
Italian arborio rice

2 cups chicken stock
3/4 cup frozen peas
1 packet Sazón Goya Seasoning with
Saffron, dissolved in 2 tablespoons
hot water
Coarse sea salt and freshly
ground pepper to taste
6 shrimp, peeled
8 fresh mussels in shells, debearded
and cleaned
1/2 to 1 cup chicken stock
1 tablespoon chopped fresh parsley

Sauté the monkfish and squid in 2 tablespoons olive oil in a paella pan or large skillet over high
heat for 3 minutes. Remove the monkfish, squid and juices to a bowl. Sauté the onion, garlic and bell
pepper in 2 tablespoons olive oil in the paella pan over medium heat for 4 to 5 minutes or until the
onion is translucent. Stir in the tomatoes. Sauté for 2 minutes. Add the rice, 2 cups chicken stock, the
peas and seasoning mix in the order listed, mixing well after each addition. Season with salt and pepper.

Arrange the monkfish, squid, shrimp and mussels on the rice mixture. Pour the reserved juices over
the mixture. Simmer over medium-low heat for 15 minutes or until all of the liquid is absorbed. Add
1/2 cup chicken stock. Simmer for 15 minutes or until the rice is tender, adding additional chicken
stock if all of the liquid is absorbed.

Remove from the heat and let stand, covered, for 10 minutes. Discard any mussels that have not
opened. Garnish with parsley and serve warm.

Yield: 4 servings

CARAMELIZED SCALLOPS WITH MANDARIN ORANGES

The mandarin oranges add fresh sweetness to this tasty seafood dish.

CAULIFLOWER PURÉE
1 head cauliflower, cut into florets, stem peeled and cut into 1/2-inch pieces
Salt and freshly ground pepper to taste
2 to 3 tablespoons unsalted butter

SCALLOPS
2 tablespoons extra-virgin olive oil
2 tablespoons unsalted butter

1 pound bay scallops or sea scallops (thawed, if using frozen)
Salt and freshly ground pepper to taste
1 (8- or 11-ounce) can mandarin oranges, drained
1 1/2 tablespoons capers, drained
1 tablespoon finely chopped fresh Italian parsley

For the purée, combine the cauliflower with boiling salted water in a medium saucepan. Boil for 7 to 8 minutes or just until the cauliflower is tender when pierced with the tip of a knife; drain well. Purée the cauliflower in a food processor until smooth. Season with salt and pepper. Add the butter and pulse until combined; do not overwork. Spoon the mixture into a bowl and press plastic wrap directly on the surface; keep warm. You may prepare to this point and store in the refrigerator until ready to serve. Reheat before serving.

For the scallops, heat the olive oil and butter in a large skillet over medium heat. Pat the scallops dry with a paper towel and season with salt and pepper. Add the scallops to the skillet. Fry the scallops for 4 to 5 minutes for bay scallops or for 6 to 8 minutes for sea scallops or until light brown on all sides. Remove the scallops to a warm plate using a slotted spoon. Heat the butter over medium to high heat until the butter begins to brown. Add the mandarin oranges and capers and season with salt and pepper. Sauté for 1 minute or until heated through.

To serve, divide the cauliflower purée among four dinner plates. Arrange the scallops around the edge of the purée. Spoon the mandarin orange mixture over the scallops. Drizzle with the browned butter and sprinkle with the parsley. Serve immediately.

Yield: 4 servings

GARLIC SHRIMP PENNE WITH CILANTRO CREAM

Prepare this dish for your family as an easy weeknight meal.

1 garlic bulb
2 teaspoons olive oil
1/4 cup chicken broth
1/2 cup evaporated milk
1 tablespoon cornstarch
1 tablespoon water
1/2 teaspoon each salt and pepper
2 tablespoons fresh cilantro
16 ounces penne
1 teaspoon olive oil
8 ounces small shrimp, peeled and deveined
1 cup (4 ounces) grated Parmesan cheese

Preheat the oven to 375 degrees. Cut the garlic into halves horizontally, leaving the skin on. Place the garlic halves cut side up on aluminum foil. Coat the garlic with 2 teaspoons olive oil. Fold the aluminum foil around the garlic to enclose. Roast for 45 minutes.

Remove the skin from the garlic and combine the garlic with the chicken broth in a small saucepan. Bring to a boil. Add the evaporated milk. Bring to a boil. Remove from the heat. Dissolve the cornstarch in the water in a small bowl. Add the cornstarch mixture, salt, pepper and cilantro to the sauce. Spoon the sauce into a blender and process until smooth.

Cook the pasta to al dente using the package directions; drain. Sauté the shrimp in 1 teaspoon olive oil in a large skillet until pink. Add the sauce and Parmesan cheese and mix well. Add the pasta and mix well. Serve immediately. You may substitute chopped boneless chicken for the shrimp if desired.

Yield: 4 to 6 servings

SHRIMP AND FETA BAKED ZITI

This Greek-style pasta dish makes a great dinner party entrée.

1 onion, thinly sliced
2 tablespoons olive oil
2 large garlic cloves, thinly sliced
3 cups chopped drained canned plum tomatoes
2 teaspoons minced fresh oregano, or 1 teaspoon dried oregano
1/2 teaspoon red pepper flakes
Salt and freshly ground pepper to taste
2 tablespoons minced fresh basil
16 ounces large shrimp, peeled and deveined
12 ounces ziti, cooked and drained
1/4 cup minced fresh parsley
8 ounces feta cheese, crumbled

Preheat the oven to 400 degrees. Cook the onion in the olive oil in a large saucepan over medium heat for 4 minutes, stirring occasionally. Add the garlic and cook for 3 to 4 minutes or until the onion and garlic are golden brown, stirring occasionally.

Add the tomatoes, oregano, red pepper flakes, salt and pepper and mix well. Simmer for 6 to 8 minutes or until thickened, stirring occasionally. Add the basil and shrimp. Cook for 1 to 2 minutes or just until the shrimp are pink, stirring gently.

Combine the pasta, shrimp mixture, half of the parsley and half the feta cheese in a large bowl and stir gently. Spoon into an oiled shallow 3-quart baking dish. Sprinkle with the remaining parsley and feta cheese. Bake, loosely covered with aluminum foil, for 20 minutes or until bubbly. Remove the foil and broil until golden brown.

Yield: 4 to 6 servings

ROASTED VEGETABLE PASTA

A hearty vegetarian dish that showcases eggplant and red bell peppers.
For a nonvegetarian version, add chopped roasted chicken.

1 eggplant, cubed	2 tablespoons olive oil
2 tablespoons olive oil	16 ounces miniature penne
Salt and pepper to taste	1 tablespoon olive oil
Juice of 2 lemons	1 bunch basil, stemmed and
2 red bell peppers	cut into chiffonade

Preheat the oven to 350 degrees. Combine the eggplant and 2 tablespoons olive oil in a bowl and toss gently. Season with salt and pepper. Place the eggplant in a roasting pan. Roast until golden brown and tender. Toss the eggplant with 2 tablespoons of the lemon juice in a bowl. Combine the bell peppers with 2 tablespoons olive oil in a bowl and toss gently. Season with salt and pepper. Place the red peppers in a roasting pan. Roast until the skin is blackened and blistered. Let stand until cool. Remove and discard the skins, seeds and stems, reserving the juices. Julienne the bell pepper flesh.

Cook the pasta to al dente using the package directions; drain. Toss the pasta with 1 tablespoon olive oil, salt and pepper in a bowl. Add the eggplant, bell peppers, reserved bell pepper juices and basil and toss gently. Adjust the seasonings to taste, adding additional lemon juice and olive oil if desired. Serve immediately.

Yield: 6 to 8 servings

DARE TO BE BARE

Put away the tablecloths and placemats, and show off
the gorgeous wood grain of your bare table. This tablesetting
tactic also draws more attention to the food and floral
arrangement. You may still choose to use small plate
coasters to protect your table.

VODKA TOMATO RIGATONI

Feel free to try other pasta shapes with this magnificent sauce.

2 tablespoons butter
1 small onion, chopped
2 garlic cloves, minced
1 tablespoon dried Italian seasoning
1 (14- or 16-ounce) can Italian plum
tomatoes, chopped and juices reserved
3 ounces prosciutto, sliced
1/4 cup vodka, or more to taste
3/4 cup whipping cream
1/2 cup (2 ounces) grated Parmesan cheese
8 ounces rigatoni or other tubular pasta, cooked and drained
Salt and pepper to taste
Grated Parmesan cheese

Melt the butter in a heavy skillet over medium high heat. Add the onion, garlic and Italian seasonings and sauté for 4 minutes or until the onion is translucent. Add the tomatoes with the reserved juices and prosciutto and simmer for 10 minutes, stirring occasionally.

Add the vodka and simmer for 5 minutes, stirring occasionally. Add the cream and 1/2 cup Parmesan cheese and simmer for 4 minutes or until slightly thickened, stirring occasionally. Add the pasta and stir to coat with the sauce. Season with salt and pepper. Serve with Parmesan cheese.

Yield: 2 generous servings

MUSHROOM FRITTATA

A frittata can be served for breakfast, brunch, or even a casual dinner.
For a twist, try it with scallions, bacon, or asparagus.

2 tablespoons butter	6 eggs
1 onion, chopped	1 cup whipping cream
1 green bell pepper, chopped	1/4 cup milk
1 red bell pepper, chopped	1 1/4 teaspoons salt
4 large mushrooms, chopped	1/4 teaspoon ground cumin
4 ounces mild Cheddar,	1/4 teaspoon dried thyme
cheese shredded	Dash of pepper
	2 dashes Tabasco sauce

Preheat the oven to 325 degrees. Melt the butter in a heavy skillet over medium heat. Add the onion, bell peppers and mushrooms and sauté for 7 minutes or until the vegetables are tender, stirring frequently. Press the cheese evenly over the bottom and side of a buttered 8-cup baking dish.

Beat the eggs, cream, milk, salt, cumin, thyme, pepper and Tabasco sauce in a bowl until blended. Add all but 1/3 cup of the vegetable mixture and mix well. Spoon into the prepared baking dish. Bake for 30 minutes or until almost set in the center. Sprinkle with the remaining 1/3 cup vegetable mixture. Bake for 10 minutes longer.

Yield: 6 to 8 servings

A HOPPING GOOD HUNT

If you're planning a neighborhood Easter egg hunt, be sure to plan

separate areas according to age. For example, have a smaller "3 and

under" area with easy-to-see eggs; a larger "4- to 6-year-old"

section with slightly hidden eggs; and a more challenging "7 and up"

area. Use wooden stakes and ropes to segment each "huntscape."

FINISHING TOUCHES

GUAVA RUM CHEESECAKE

The rich flavor of cream cheese and light guava flavoring are sure to soothe the palate.

1/3 cup melted butter	2 cups sugar
2 tablespoons sugar	4 eggs
1 1/4 cups graham cracker crumbs	1 tablespoon lemon zest
1 cup guava paste	2 teaspoons vanilla extract
1/3 cup rum	1/4 cup guava jelly
32 ounces cream cheese, softened	1 tablespoon water

Preheat the oven to 350 degrees. Combine the butter, 2 tablespoons sugar and the graham cracker crumbs in a bowl and mix well. Press the mixture over the bottom and up the side of a buttered 9-inch springform pan. Bake for 8 minutes. Let stand until cool.

Melt the guava paste in a saucepan over low heat. Stir vigorously for 2 to 3 minutes or until smooth. Stir in the rum. Remove from the heat and let stand until cool. Beat the cream cheese in a large mixing bowl until light and fluffy. Add 2 cups sugar and beat until blended. Beat in the eggs one at a time. Add the lemon zest and vanilla and mix well. Fold in the guava mixture gently. Pour into the prepared crust. Bake for 1 1/4 hours, tenting with foil if the top begins to brown. Turn off the oven and let the cheesecake cool in the oven for 20 minutes. Chill for 6 to 8 hours. Heat the guava jelly and water in a small saucepan until the mixture is the consistency of heavy cream, stirring constantly. Let stand until cool. Brush over the cheesecake. Chill, covered, for 30 minutes or longer before serving.

Yield: 12 generous servings

GUAVA HISTORY

Grown throughout the tropical Americas, guava is one of the most common fruits in the world. Its sweet pulp is used in a variety of drinks, desserts, and other food products. Guava was reportedly introduced to south Florida in 1847 and was common to more than half the state by 1886. Guava paste and jelly can be found in Latino grocery stores and some local supermarkets.

CHOCOLATE AMARETTO CHEESECAKE WITH RASPBERRY AMARETTO SAUCE

The perfect blend of flavors makes this cheesecake a truly special and elegant treat.

RASPBERRY AMARETTO SAUCE
1 cup raspberries
1/4 cup confectioners' sugar, or more to taste
6 tablespoons amaretto
2 teaspoons lemon juice

CHEESECAKE
1 cup graham cracker crumbs
1/2 cup (1 stick) butter, melted

1 cup (6 ounces) chocolate chips
1 cup heavy cream
2 tablespoons butter
8 ounces cream cheese
4 egg yolks
1 (14-ounce) can sweetened condensed milk
1/4 cup amaretto
1 teaspoon almond extract

For the sauce, combine the raspberries, confectioners' sugar, liqueur and lemon juice in a food processor and process until smooth, adding additional confectioners' sugar if needed. Strain into a bowl and chill, covered, until ready to serve.

For the cheesecake, preheat the oven to 350 degrees. Combine the graham cracker crumbs and 1/2 cup butter in a bowl and mix until the graham cracker crumbs are moistened. Press the mixture into a 9-inch pie pan. Bake for 10 minutes. Let stand until cool. Place the chocolate chips in a small saucepan over medium-low heat. Add the cream slowly and stir until smooth and creamy. Whisk in 2 tablespoons butter. Remove from the heat.

Beat the cream cheese in a mixing bowl until smooth. Add the egg yolks one at a time, beating well after each addition. Add the condensed milk, liqueur and almond extract and beat until smooth, stopping to scrape down the side of the bowl as needed. Spoon some of the chocolate sauce into the prepared crust. Let stand for 2 to 3 minutes. Pour the cream cheese mixture over the chocolate sauce. Drizzle rows of the chocolate sauce over the cream cheese mixture, reserving some of the chocolate sauce. Swirl the mixtures together using a wooden pick or skewer. Bake for 30 to 40 minutes or until the cheesecake is set. Chill in the refrigerator. Spoon the raspberry sauce onto dessert plates. Cut the cheesecake into wedges and place on the raspberry sauce. Drizzle the reserved chocolate sauce on the cheesecake.

Yield: 8 servings

MARBLED PUMPKIN CHEESECAKE WITH GINGERSNAP CRUMB CRUST

The perfect alternative to traditional pumpkin pie. A gingersnap crust
is a great way to spice up a cheesecake.

GINGERSNAP CRUMB CRUST
1 1/2 cups finely ground gingersnaps
1/3 cup sugar
5 tablespoons unsalted butter, melted
1/8 teaspoon salt

CHEESECAKE
24 ounces cream cheese, softened
1 3/4 cups sugar

3 tablespoons all-purpose flour
5 eggs
1/2 teaspoon vanilla extract
2 egg yolks
1 (15-ounce) can pumpkin
3/4 teaspoon ground cinnamon
1/8 teaspoon ground ginger
1/8 teaspoon ground allspice
1/8 teaspoon freshly grated nutmeg

For the crust, combine the gingersnap crumbs, sugar, butter and salt in a bowl and mix well. Press onto the bottom and one inch up the side of a buttered 10-inch springform pan. Can be prepared in advance and chilled for up to 2 hours.

For the cheesecake, preheat the oven to 550 degrees. Combine the cream cheese, sugar and flour in a mixing bowl and beat until smooth. Add the eggs one at a time, beating on low after each addition. Beat in the vanilla. Spoon 2 1/2 cups of the mixture into a bowl. Beat the egg yolks, pumpkin, cinnamon, ginger, allspice and nutmeg into the remaining cream cheese mixture. Place the springform pan into a shallow baking pan. Pour half of the pumpkin mixture into the prepared pan. Top with half of the reserved cream cheese mixture. Repeat the procedure with the remaining pumpkin mixture and cream cheese mixture, drizzling the cream cheese mixture over the top. The springform pan will be completely full. Swirl the mixtures once in a figure-eight pattern using a spoon and being careful not to touch the side of the pan or the crust.

Bake on the middle rack of the oven for 12 minutes or until puffed. Reduce the oven temperature to 200 degrees and bake for 30 minutes. Do not open the oven. Tent the cheesecake with a lightly oiled piece of aluminum foil and bake for 1 hour longer or just until firm. Run a knife around the edge of the pan to loosen and cool completely in the pan on a wire rack. Chill, loosely covered, for 6 hours or longer. Bring to room temperature before serving.

Yield: 16 servings

DEVILISHLY DELICIOUS DIRT

*Kids will love to sink their hands into this yucky (we mean yummy!)
dessert on Halloween. Or, you can serve it in a flower pot with candy flowers for a
spring birthday party, and watch kids delight as their imaginations bloom.*

8 ounces cream cheese, softened
1/2 cup (1 stick) butter, softened
1 cup confectioners' sugar
3 cups milk
2 cups heavy whipping cream, whipped

2 (4-ounce) packages vanilla instant
pudding mix
1 package chocolate sandwich
cookies, crushed
Gummy worms

Combine the cream cheese, butter and confectioners' sugar in a mixing bowl and beat until blended. Add the milk, whipped cream and pudding mix and beat until smooth. Alternate layers of the crushed cookies and the pudding mixture in a serving dish, ending with the crushed cookies. Chill until ready to serve. Decorate with gummy worms.

Yield: 10 to 12 servings

RASPBERRY LEMON GRANITA

*A light, refreshing way to end a summertime meal. Garnish with fresh raspberries or mint
leaves. For a different flavor, substitute the lemon juice with another fruit juice.*

1/2 cup water
1/2 cup sugar
1 cup (1/2 pint) fresh raspberries
1/2 cup lemon juice

11/2 cups water
Sparkling water, chilled
Fresh raspberries or mint leaves

Combine 1/2 cup water and the sugar in a small saucepan and cook over high heat until the sugar is dissolved, stirring constantly. Remove from the heat. Pass the raspberries through a food mill fitted with a fine disk or press through a fine sieve into a bowl, discarding the solids. Whisk the sugar syrup, lemon juice and 11/2 cups water into the raspberry purée. Pour into a freezer-safe serving dish and freeze until solid. Scrape the granita into martini glasses using a spoon. Pour a dash of sparkling water on each serving. Garnish with fresh raspberries or mint.

Yield: 6 cups

BUTTERSCOTCH POACHED PEARS

Let this elegant dessert be the grand finale at your next dinner party.

1 cup packed light brown sugar
1/4 cup (1/2 stick) butter
1/4 cup light corn syrup
1/4 teaspoon salt
2 teaspoons vanilla extract
1/2 cup heavy cream
1 (750-milliliter) bottle good-quality white wine
1 1/2 cups granulated sugar
1 cinnamon stick
1 (2-inch) strip lemon zest
2 tablespoons lemon juice
6 cloves
6 firm ripe Bosc pears

Combine the brown sugar, butter, corn syrup and salt in a small saucepan over medium-low heat. Cook for 3 minutes or until the butter is melted and the mixture is blended, stirring constantly. Increase the heat to medium-high and bring the mixture to a gentle boil. Boil for 2 minutes, stirring frequently. Remove from the heat and stir in the vanilla and cream. Let stand until cool. Chill, covered, for 1 hour or until thickened.

Combine the wine, granulated sugar, cinnamon stick, lemon zest, lemon juice and cloves in a large saucepan. Bring to a boil and boil for 5 minutes or until the sugar is dissolved, stirring frequently. Peel the pears vertically from the stem down, leaving the stem intact. Remove the core from the bottom of the pears. Add the pears to the wine mixture and reduce the heat. Simmer, covered, for 10 to 15 minutes or until the pears are tender. Remove from the heat and let cool to room temperature. Spoon the sauce onto six dessert plates. Top each with a pear and pass any extra sauce.

Yield: 6 servings

PEACH RASPBERRY TRIFLE

A trifle makes a beautiful centerpiece for a dinner party dessert table.

1¹/2 cups heavy whipping cream
¹/2 cup confectioners' sugar
¹/2 teaspoon almond extract
1 pound fresh peaches, peeled and
   cut into wedges
2 tablespoons granulated sugar
Juice of ¹/2 lemon or lime
¹/2 cup sliced almonds, rinsed

¹/2 cup confectioners' sugar
1 cup fresh raspberries or strawberries
¹/4 cup raspberry jam or strawberry jam
Juice of ¹/2 lime
Rum, amaretto or apple juice
1 (10-ounce) pound cake, cut into
   1- to 2-inch cubes
¹/4 cup thinly sliced fresh mint

Beat the cream, ¹/2 cup confectioners' sugar and the almond extract in a bowl on high speed for 4 to 5 minutes or until soft peaks form. Chill until serving time. Preheat the oven to 400 degrees. Toss the peaches with the granulated sugar and lemon juice in a bowl. Toss the almonds with ¹/2 cup confectioners' sugar in a bowl. Spread the almonds on a baking sheet coated with nonstick cooking spray. Bake for 8 to 9 minutes or until golden brown, stirring once after 5 minutes. Be careful not to let them burn. Spread the almonds on parchment paper to cool. Purée the raspberries, jam and lime juice in a food processor or blender. Drizzle rum over the pound cake. Layer the peaches, pound cake and raspberry purée loosely in a trifle bowl or glass serving bowl. Top with the whipped cream. Garnish with the mint and sugared almonds. You may substitute two 8-ounce cans peaches, drained, or one 16-ounce package thawed frozen peaches for the fresh peaches.

Yield: 6 servings

TRIFLE TIP

Try some unique presentation ideas for this or other

trifles. At an intimate dinner for two, serve trifle in large wine

glasses set on a silver tray. Use plastic goblets on a colorful

tray for casual summer get-togethers.

WHITE CHOCOLATE GRAND MARNIER CREPES WITH STRAWBERRY SAUCE

A light, creamy blend of white chocolate with a hint of orange tucked into a crepe.
Make the crepes, mousse, and sauce ahead, and assemble just before serving.

1 cup heavy cream	1 cup instant blending flour or
12 ounces good-quality white	all-purpose flour
chocolate, chopped	2/3 cup cold milk
1/4 cup Grand Marnier	2/3 cup cold water
2 egg whites	3 eggs
1 cup heavy whipping cream,	1/4 teaspoon salt
whipped	3 tablespoons butter, melted
1 pound fresh strawberries, stemmed	Additional melted butter
3 tablespoons confectioners' sugar, or	Confectioners' sugar
to taste	Chocolate curls

Heat the heavy cream in a saucepan over medium-low heat until bubbles form around the edge. Remove from the heat and stir in the white chocolate until smooth. Stir in the liqueur. Pour the mixture into a bowl. Beat the egg whites in a bowl until stiff peaks form. Fold the egg whites into the cream mixture one-third at a time. Fold in the whipped cream one-third at a time. Chill, covered with plastic wrap, for 8 to 10 hours. Process the strawberries in a food processor until smooth. Pour through a fine sieve placed over a bowl, pressing to extract as much of the juice as possible. Discard the solids. Add 3 tablespoons confectioners' sugar to the strawberry juice and whisk until the confectioners' sugar is dissolved. Chill, covered, until ready to serve.

Process the flour, milk, water, eggs, salt and 3 tablespoons butter in a blender or food processor until smooth. Chill for 10 minutes if using blending flour or for 30 minutes to 8 hours if using all-purpose flour. Heat a nonstick or well-seasoned 6- to 8-inch frying pan until drops of water dance on it. Brush lightly with melted butter. Pour 2 to 3 tablespoons of the batter into the pan, tilting the pan to cover the bottom evenly. Cook for 1 minute or until brown on the bottom. Turn and cook briefly. Remove to a wire rack to cool. Repeat with the remaining batter. Stack the crepes on top of each other, placing a piece of waxed paper between each crepe. You may chill the crepes for two days or freeze for several weeks. Place a crepe on a flat work surface. Place a dollop of the mousse on the lower right quarter. Fold the right side of the crepe over the mousse. Fold the top of the crepe down. Place the crepe folded side down onto a dessert plate. Sprinkle with confectioners' sugar and pour the strawberry sauce around the crepe. Top with chocolate curls.

Yield: 6 to 8 servings

CHOCOLATE ROULADE WITH WARM CHOCOLATE SAUCE

Special occasions call for this incredible dessert, which is surprisingly light.
The hot chocolate sauce warms the filling and melts in your mouth.

ROULADE
3/4 cup confectioners' sugar
2 tablespoons flour
2 tablespoons baking cocoa
Pinch of salt
5 egg whites
5 egg yolks
2 tablespoons vanilla extract
1 cup heavy whipping cream
1/4 cup confectioners' sugar
1/2 teaspoon vanilla extract

CHOCOLATE SAUCE
6 tablespoons hot water
1 ounce unsweetened chocolate
1 teaspoon butter
1/8 teaspoons salt
3 tablespoons white corn syrup
1/2 teaspoon vanilla extract

For the roulade, preheat the oven to 400 degrees. Sift together 3/4 cup confectioners' sugar, the flour, baking cocoa and salt. Beat the egg whites in a mixing bowl until stiff peaks form. Beat the egg yolks in a bowl until light yellow and creamy. Fold the egg yolks into the egg whites. Add the sifted mixture and mix well by hand. Add 2 tablespoons vanilla and mix well. Pour the batter onto a well-greased waxed paper- or parchment-lined 10×15-inch cake pan. Bake for 7 minutes. Dust a clean kitchen towel with confectioners' sugar. Invert the cake onto the towel and roll as for a jelly roll. Let stand until cool. Whip the cream in a bowl. Add 1/4 cup confectioners' sugar and 1/2 teaspoon vanilla and mix well. Unroll the cooled cake carefully and remove the towel. Spread the cake evenly with the filling. Reroll the cake and chill in the refrigerator until ready to serve.

For the sauce, combine the water, chocolate, butter and salt in a saucepan and bring just to a boil. Add the corn syrup and boil for 5 minutes, stirring frequently. Remove from the heat and let cool slightly. Stir in the vanilla. Cut the chocolate roll into slices and spoon the warm sauce over the slices.

Yield: 6 to 8 servings

BRAZO GITANO "CIEN AÑOS"

*Baked Alaska meets strawberry shortcake in this 100th anniversary version
of the original recipe from Casimiro Hernandez, Sr., founder of
Columbia Restaurant. A sponge cake is soaked in syrup with Spanish Manzanilla
sherry and filled with ice cream and strawberries, rolled and topped with
meringue. Flambéed and served with strawberry sauce.*

5 egg yolks	1 cup water
1/2 cup sugar	1 strip lemon zest
Pinch of salt	1/2 cup dry sherry
1/3 cup cornstarch	5 egg whites
2 cups milk	1/4 teaspoon cream of tartar
1 cinnamon stick	1 cup sugar
1 teaspoon vanilla extract	3/4 cup strawberry glaze
7 egg whites	2 tablespoons water
7 egg yolks	2 pints fresh strawberries, cut into
3/4 cup sugar	quarters
1 cup cake flour, sifted	3 tablespoons kirschwasser or other
11/2 cups sugar	cherry-flavored brandy

Beat 5 egg yolks in a heavy saucepan using a wooden spoon until lemon-colored. Add 1/2 cup sugar and the salt and mix well. Dissolve the cornstarch in a small amount of the milk in a bowl. Add the cornstarch mixture and the remaining milk to the egg yolk mixture. Add the cinnamon stick and cook over medium heat until the mixture is the consistency of a heavy custard, stirring constantly. Remove from the heat and stir in the vanilla. Remove and discard the cinnamon stick. Let stand until cool.

Preheat the oven to 400 degrees. Beat 7 egg whites at high speed in a mixing bowl until soft peaks form. Add 7 egg yolks one at a time, beating well after each addition. Add 3/4 cup sugar one tablespoon at a time, beating well after each addition. Fold the flour in gradually. Pour the mixture into a waxed paper-lined 10×15-inch cake pan and bake for 12 minutes. Sprinkle a clean kitchen towel with confectioners' sugar. Invert the cake onto the kitchen towel and remove the waxed paper. Spread evenly with the custard and roll as for a jelly roll. Place on an ovenproof serving tray. Increase the oven temperature to 425 degrees.

Combine 1 1/2 cups sugar, 1 cup water and the lemon zest in a small saucepan. Bring to a boil and boil for 10 minutes, stirring frequently. Stir in the sherry. Remove the lemon zest. Pour the mixture gradually over the cake allowing it to soak into the cake. Combine 5 egg whites and the cream of tartar in a bowl and beat until soft peaks form. Add 1 cup sugar gradually, beating constantly until stiff peaks form. Spread over the cake. Bake for 6 to 8 minutes or until the meringue is light brown.

Combine the strawberry glaze and 2 tablespoons water in a bowl and mix well. Add the strawberries and stir gently to coat. Spoon over the cake. Pour the brandy over the strawberries and carefully ignite.

Yield: 12 servings

BEHIND THE RECIPE

"Brazo de Gitano translates literally as Gypsy's Arm,"
says Richard Gonzmart, fourth generation family member and
president of Columbia Restaurant. "It's a recipe from
my great grandfather, Casimiro Hernandez, and it is a dessert
my family has enjoyed during the holidays since I was born."

SUGARPLUM CAKE

Let visions of our scrumptious sugarplum cake fill your family with festive holiday cheer.

CAKE
2 cups all-purpose flour
1¹/2 cups sugar
1 teaspoon baking soda
1 teaspoon salt
1 teaspoon ground cinnamon
1 teaspoon nutmeg
1 teaspoon ground allspice
3 eggs
1 cup buttermilk

3/4 cup vegetable oil
1 cup puréed stewed prunes
1 cup chopped pecans

BUTTER PECAN ICING
1 cup sugar
1/2 cup (1 stick) butter
1 tablespoon light corn syrup
1 teaspoon baking soda
1 cup chopped pecans

For the cake, preheat the oven to 350 degrees. Sift the flour, sugar, baking soda, salt, cinnamon, nutmeg and allspice together into a large mixing bowl. Add the eggs, buttermilk, oil and prunes and beat until blended. Stir in the pecans. Pour into a greased and floured 9×13-inch cake pan. Bake for 40 minutes.

For the icing, combine the sugar, butter, corn syrup and baking soda in a saucepan and cook over medium heat to 234 to 240 degrees on a candy thermometer, soft-ball stage, stirring constantly. Remove from the heat and let cool slightly. Add the pecans and beat until the mixture is of spreading consistency. Spread over the cooled cake.

Yield: 12 servings

SWEETHEART RED VELVET CAKE

*Red is the color of romance—let this luscious cake be the finishing
touch to an intimate evening with the one you love.*

CAKE
1/2 cup (1 stick) butter, softened
1 1/2 cups sugar
2 eggs
2 tablespoons baking cocoa
2 ounces red food coloring
1 cup buttermilk
1 teaspoon vanilla extract
1 teaspoon salt
2 1/2 cups all-purpose flour

1 tablespoon vinegar
1 1/2 teaspoons baking soda

VANILLA FROSTING
5 tablespoons sifted all-purpose flour
1 cup milk
1 cup (2 sticks) butter or margarine,
   softened
1 cup sugar
1 teaspoon vanilla extract

For the cake, preheat the oven to 350 degrees. Cream the butter, sugar and eggs in a mixing bowl until light and fluffy. Combine the baking cocoa and food coloring in a small bowl and stir until of a paste consistency. Add to the creamed mixture and mix well. Combine the buttermilk, vanilla and salt in a bowl and mix well. Add to the creamed mixture alternately with the flour, beating well after each addition. Stir the vinegar and baking soda together in a small bowl. Fold into the buttermilk mixture. Do not beat. Pour into two greased and floured 9-inch round cake pans or 9-inch heart-shaped cake pans. Bake for 30 minutes. Cool in the pans for 15 minutes. Remove to a wire rack to cool completely.

For the frosting, combine the flour and milk in a saucepan over medium heat and cook until thickened, stirring constantly. Remove from the heat and let stand until completely cool. Cream the butter, sugar and vanilla in a mixing bowl. Add to the milk mixture and beat until of a spreading consistency. Spread between the layers and over the top and side of the cake.

Yield: 12 servings

WARM RASPBERRY CHOCOLATE CAKE

*This sinfully delicious cake actually frosts itself—the chocolate
frosting is cooked in the bottom of the cake pan.*

3 ounces semisweet chocolate, chopped
1/2 cup seedless raspberry jam
1/2 cup heavy cream
1/3 cup plus 1 tablespoon baking cocoa
1/2 cup boiling water
1/4 cup milk
1/2 teaspoon vanilla extract
1/3 cup seedless raspberry jam

1/2 cup (1 stick) butter, softened
1/3 cup packed brown sugar
1/3 cup granulated sugar
2 eggs
1 cup all-purpose flour
3/4 teaspoon baking soda
1/4 teaspoon salt
Raspberries

Preheat the oven to 350 degrees. Combine the chocolate, 1/2 cup jam and the cream in a small heavy saucepan and bring to a simmer, stirring constantly until smooth. Pour into a buttered 9-inch cake pan.

Combine the baking cocoa and water in a bowl and mix well. Add the milk, vanilla and 1/3 cup jam and mix well. Cream the butter, brown sugar and granulated sugar in a mixing bowl until light and fluffy. Add the eggs one at a time, beating well after each addition. Combine the flour, baking soda and salt in a bowl. Add to the creamed mixture alternately with the jam mixture, beating well after each addition. Pour evenly over the chocolate mixture in the cake pan. Bake for 30 to 35 minutes or until a wooden pick inserted in the center comes out clean. Cool in the pan for 10 to 20 minutes. Run a knife around the edge and invert onto a serving platter. Garnish with raspberries. You may prepare one day in advance. Do not invert onto the serving platter. Let stand, covered, at room temperature in the cake pan. Reheat, uncovered, at 350 degrees for 10 to 15 minutes and serve as directed.

Yield: 6 to 8 servings

APPLE CRANBERRY PIE

Put a twist on the traditional holiday gathering by serving this delightful dessert à la mode.

3/4 cup packed brown sugar
1/4 cup granulated sugar
1/3 cup all-purpose flour
1 teaspoon ground cinnamon
4 cups sliced peeled tart apples, such as Granny Smith
2 cups fresh cranberries
1 unbaked (9-inch) pie shell
1/3 cup butter, softened
1/2 cup granulated sugar
3/4 cup all-purpose flour

Preheat the oven to 425 degrees. Combine the brown sugar, 1/4 cup granulated sugar, 1/3 cup flour and the cinnamon in a bowl. Add the apples and cranberries and toss gently to coat. Spoon into the pie shell. Combine the butter, 1/2 cup granulated sugar and 3/4 cup flour in a bowl and mix until crumbly. Sprinkle evenly over the apples and cranberries. Bake, loosely covered with aluminum foil, for 45 minutes.

Yield: 8 servings

MAKE IT A LA MODE

A dollop of your favorite frozen treat adds a layer of refreshing flavor to many pies and cakes. For variations on traditional vanilla, try cinnamon ice cream on apple pie, coffee ice cream on rum cake, or peppermint stick ice cream on pumpkin pie.

COCONUT CREAM PIE

This traditional custard dessert includes three parts: crust, custard, and topping.
Though the custard takes some time to set, the result is well worth the wait.

1¹/4 cups sweetened flaked coconut
1/2 (7-ounce) package shortbread
cookies, crushed
1/2 cup (1 stick) unsalted butter, melted
1/2 cup plus 1 tablespoon
granulated sugar
3 tablespoons cornstarch

1/4 teaspoon salt
2¹/4 cups milk
3 egg yolks
3 tablespoons unsalted butter, chilled
3/4 cup heavy whipping cream
1 tablespoon confectioners' sugar

Preheat the oven to 350 degrees. Spread the coconut evenly in a baking sheet with sides. Bake for 8 to 10 minutes or until golden brown, stirring once. Remove from the oven and let stand until cool. Process the cookie crumbs, 1/2 cup butter and 1/4 cup of the coconut in a food processor until finely ground and the mixture just begins to hold together. Press evenly over the bottom and up the side of a 9-inch glass pie pan. Bake for 10 minutes or until golden brown. Let stand until cool.

Whisk the granulated sugar, cornstarch and salt together in a saucepan over medium heat. Add the the milk and egg yolks, whisking until well combined. Bring the mixture to a boil, whisking constantly. Remove from the heat and add the butter, whisking until the butter is melted and the mixture is blended. Stir in 3/4 cup of the remaining coconut. Spoon the mixture into the pie shell and smooth the top. Press plastic wrap onto the custard and chill for 2 to 3 hours or until firm.

Beat the cream and confectioners' sugar in a chilled large stainless steel bowl for 2 to 3 minutes or until stiff peaks form. Spread the whipped cream over the custard layer. Sprinkle with the remaining 1/4 cup coconut.

Yield: 12 servings

CHOCOLATE PECAN TART WITH CARAMEL SAUCE

An amazingly delicious tart version of the chocolate chip cookie, this dessert is best served à la mode. For a yummy twist, top with butter pecan ice cream instead of vanilla.

TART
3 cups all-purpose flour
1 teaspoon baking soda
1/2 teaspoon baking powder
1 teaspoon salt
1 cup (2 sticks) unsalted butter, softened
1 cup packed light brown sugar
1 cup granulated sugar
2 eggs

2 teaspoons vanilla extract
2 1/2 cups (15 ounces) chocolate chips
1 cup pecans, toasted and chopped

CARAMEL SAUCE
1 1/2 cups granulated sugar
1 cup heavy cream
6 tablespoons unsalted butter
1 teaspoon vanilla extract
Pinch of salt

For the tart, preheat the oven to 350 degrees. Combine the flour, baking soda, baking powder and salt in a bowl. Cream the butter, brown sugar and granulated sugar in a mixing bowl until light and fluffy. Add the eggs and vanilla and beat until blended. Add the flour mixture and mix well. The mixture will be very thick. Stir in the chocolate chips and pecans. Spread into a 9-inch tart pan with a removable bottom that has been sprayed with nonstick baking spray. There will be some of the mixture left over. You may make cookies from the mixture. Place the filled tart pan on a baking sheet and bake for 25 to 35 minutes or until the top is golden brown and firm. Let cool for 1 hour.

For the sauce, cook the granulated sugar in a 2 1/2- to 3-quart heavy saucepan over medium to medium-high heat until it begins to melt. Do not stir. Cook until the sugar is melted and a deep caramel color, stirring occasionally. Remove from the heat and carefully pour the cream into the saucepan. The sugar will harden and the mixture will steam. Return to the heat and cook until the sugar has softened, stirring frequently. Reduce the heat and stir in the butter, vanilla and salt. Cook until the butter is melted and the mixture is heated through, stirring frequently. Pour the warm sauce over the tart. You may store the sauce in the refrigerator for up to a week. Reheat slowly before serving.

Yield: 10 servings

BROWNIE MINT SQUARES

Cool things down this summer with this minty chocolate dessert—perfect for a pool party or picnic.

1 cup (2 sticks) butter (do not use margarine)	1/2 cup (1 stick) butter, softened
4 ounces unsweetened chocolate	4 cups confectioners' sugar
4 eggs	1/4 cup crème de menthe
2 cups granulated sugar	1/4 cup half-and-half
1 cup all-purpose flour	1/4 cup (1/2 stick) butter
1 teaspoon vanilla extract	1 cup (6 ounces) chocolate chips
1/2 teaspoon salt	3 tablespoons water

Heat 1 cup butter and the unsweetened chocolate in a saucepan over medium-low heat until the butter and chocolate are melted, stirring frequently. Let stand until cool. Preheat the oven to 350 degrees. Mix the chocolate mixture with the eggs, granulated sugar, flour, vanilla and salt in a bowl. Pour into a 9×13-inch baking pan and bake for 30 minutes. Mix 1/2 cup butter, the confectioners' sugar, crème de menthe and half-and-half in a bowl. Spread over the brownie layer. Refrigerate until completely chilled. Heat 1/4 cup butter, the chocolate chips and water in a small saucepan over medium-low heat until the butter and chocolate are melted, stirring frequently. Pour over the mint layer. Refrigerate until chilled. Cut into small squares to serve.

Yield: 24 squares

PIECE OF CAKE PEPPERMINT PIE

For a holiday dessert ready before you can say, "Saint Nick," thaw

a carton of peppermint ice cream, mix it with a container of whipped

cream, and pour it into a chocolate pie crust. Freeze for several hours.

Drizzle with chocolate syrup, and sprinkle with crushed peppermint

candies. For an autumn version, use peanut butter cup ice cream, and

sprinkle with crumbled Reese's Peanut Butter Cups.

RASPBERRY CRUMB BARS

*A butter cookie on the bottom, tart raspberry filling, and a rich crumb topping
make a sweet treat for a shower, tea, or afternoon snack.*

2 cups all-purpose flour
1/2 teaspoon baking powder
1/2 teaspoon salt
3/4 cup (11/2 sticks) unsalted
butter, softened
1 cup granulated sugar
1 egg
1/2 teaspoon vanilla extract
3/4 cup good-quality raspberry preserves

1 cup fresh raspberries, or 1 cup frozen
raspberries, thawed and drained
1 tablespoon Chambord (optional)
1 cup plus 2 tablespoons
all-purpose flour
3/4 cup confectioners' sugar
1/2 teaspoon salt
6 tablespoons unsalted butter, chopped

Preheat the oven to 375 degrees. Spray a 9×13-inch baking pan with nonstick baking spray. Line the pan with aluminum foil or parchment paper, allowing excess to extend over the edges of the pan. Spray the foil with nonstick baking spray.

Combine 2 cups flour, the baking powder and 1/2 teaspoon salt in a bowl. Cream 3/4 cup butter and the granulated sugar in a mixing bowl for 2 to 3 minutes or until light and fluffy. Add the egg and vanilla and beat until blended. Add the flour mixture and mix just until the flour mixture is incorporated into the creamed mixture. The mixture will be sticky. Spread the mixture evenly over the bottom of the prepared pan using lightly oiled hands or a piece of plastic wrap to hold the mixture. Bake for 20 minutes or until light brown and set. Cool completely on a wire rack.

Combine the preserves, raspberries and liqueur in a bowl and mix gently. Spread evenly over the cooled crust. Combine 1 cup plus 2 tablespoons flour, the confectioners' sugar and 1/2 teaspoon salt in a food processor. Add 6 tablespoons butter and pulse until the mixture resembles coarse crumbs. Or combine the dry ingredients in a bowl and cut in the butter using two knives or mix with your hands. Sprinkle over the raspberry layer and bake for 20 minutes or until golden brown. Let cool completely. Lift from the pan using the foil as handles. Cut into bars.

Yield: 30 bars

HOLIDAY RASPBERRY COOKIES

An old-time favorite that makes a great gift during the holidays.

2 cups (4 sticks) margarine, softened	5 cups unsifted all-purpose flour
1 cup granulated sugar	1 egg white, beaten
1 egg	Raspberry preserves
1 egg yolk	Confectioners' sugar
1 teaspoon vanilla extract	

Preheat the oven to 350 degrees. Cream the margarine in a mixing bowl. Beat in the granulated sugar until light and fluffy. Add the egg, egg yolk and vanilla and beat until blended. Sift the flour into the mixture and mix well. Roll or pat the dough on a floured work surface. Cut with a cookie cutter and place on a baking sheet. Bake for 12 to 15 minutes or until golden brown. Let cool on the pan for 5 minutes. Remove to a wire rack to cool completely. Spread preserves over half the cookies. Top with the remaining cookies. Sprinkle with confectioners' sugar.

Yield: 4 dozen cookies

BEST-EVER GINGERSNAPS

Great for the holidays, this is a fantastic cookie recipe for busy mothers or anyone on the go. Shape the dough into balls, roll in sugar, freeze in plastic bags, and bake straight from the freezer.

2 cups all-purpose flour	1/2 teaspoon salt
1 cup sugar	3/4 cup (11/2 sticks) butter
1 teaspoon ground cinnamon	1/4 cup molasses
1 teaspoon ground ginger	1 egg, lightly beaten
1/2 teaspoon ground cloves	Sugar
1 teaspoon baking soda	

Preheat the oven to 350 degrees. Combine the flour, sugar, cinnamon, ginger, cloves, baking soda and salt in a bowl. Cut in the butter until the mixture resembles coarse crumbs. Stir in the molasses and egg. Shape the dough into 3/4- to 1-inch balls. Roll the dough balls in sugar and arrange on an ungreased cookie sheet. Bake for 12 to 15 minutes or until brown. Remove to a wire rack immediately to cool.

Yield: 41/2 dozen cookies

PUMPKIN DIP

*This yummy dip is easy to make and great served with our
Best-Ever Gingersnaps (page 116).*

16 ounces cream cheese, softened
1 (15-ounce) can pumpkin
4 cups confectioners' sugar
2 teaspoons ground cinnamon
1 teaspoon ground ginger

Combine the cream cheese, pumpkin, confectioners' sugar, cinnamon and ginger in a bowl and
beat until blended and smooth. Chill, covered, for 1 to 2 hours before serving. Serve with gingersnaps.

Yield: 8 cups

GRAVEYARD GOODIES

*For a "spooktacular" serving idea, spread Pumpkin Dip in
a rectangular serving dish and place gingersnaps in rows in the dip
to resemble tombstones in a graveyard. Use black decorator
icing to write scary sayings, such as R.I.P., on the gingersnaps.
We think this is perfect for a Halloween street party.*

PEANUT BUTTER TREATS

*Can't decide if you want cookies or candy? These scrumptious treats combine crunchy peanuts
and cereal with smooth, creamy chocolate. Great for school parties and birthdays!*

1 cup light corn syrup	6 cups corn flakes cereal
1/2 cup granulated sugar	1 cup coarsely chopped salted peanuts
1/2 cup packed brown sugar	1 (7-ounce) bar milk chocolate, melted
1 cup peanut butter	

Line a 9×13-inch pan with aluminum foil, allowing excess to extend over the edges of the pan.
Combine the corn syrup, granulated sugar and brown sugar in a 3-quart saucepan. Bring just to a boil
over medium heat, stirring frequently. Remove from the heat and stir in the peanut butter until smooth.
Add the cereal and peanuts and stir gently until coated. Spoon the mixture into the prepared pan and
press firmly. Spread with the melted chocolate. Let stand until cool, chilling in the refrigerator if
needed for the chocolate to set. Lift from the pan using the foil as handles and cut into small squares.

Yield: 30 to 45 treats

WHITE CHOCOLATE PARTY MIX

*A wickedly good treat that also makes a great party favor for any time of year.
Change your packaging to reflect the season you wish to celebrate.*

1 pound white chocolate	2 cups pretzel sticks
3 cups rice Chex cereal	2 cups dry-roasted peanuts
3 cups corn Chex cereal	1 (12-ounce) package "M&M's"
3 cups Cheerios cereal	Chocolate Candies

Melt the white chocolate in the top of a double boiler set over simmering water, stirring frequently.
Combine the cereals, pretzels, peanuts and chocolate candies in a large bowl. Pour the white chocolate
over the mixture slowly and stir gently until evenly coated. Spread the mixture on waxed paper and let
stand until cool. Break into small pieces. Store in an airtight container in the refrigerator.

Yield: 12 to 14 cups

The Perfect Setting

When setting a formal table, there is a reason for all the pomp and circumstance. China, silverware, and glassware are set to not only welcome guests to the table, but also to guide them through the meal. A few simple guidelines will help you set a proper table.

GLASSES

Set each place with every glass to be used during the dinner, with the exception of dessert. Water glasses are set to the right of the plate, just above the knife. Champagne and wine glasses belong to the right of water glasses in order of use. Bring out dessert wine glasses with the dessert.

CHINA

According to table etiquette, the bread plate and charger are the only two pieces of china included in the setting. Salad plates, dinner plates, and other serving pieces are placed on the table at the time of service. The purpose of a charger is purely decorative, and food should not be served on it directly. You may, however, set a soup bowl or salad plate on a charger, but it should be cleared before the main course.

SILVERWARE

Think "outside in" when setting your table's silverware. Consider the order in which each piece will be used and set accordingly. On the far left is the fork for the first course, while the knife for the first course is the one positioned farthest to the right. Place soup spoons, or others to be used before dessert, to the right of the knives. The dessert silverware belongs horizontally above the plate and may be added when dessert is served.

SAVORING THE SEASONS
IN OUR COMMUNITY

All through the year, The Junior League of Tampa seeks to provide our community's children and families with the building blocks essential for their physical, intellectual, emotional, and social well-being. Our more than 1,600 women exceed 80,000 volunteer service hours annually to support these goals. Each season brings new opportunities to help others.

New Beginnings   Our Kids' Connect volunteers team up with community agencies to help children waiting to be adopted find permanent homes. Each year, we hold two events where foster children and parents wishing to adopt can interact in a friendly atmosphere of games, food, prizes, and fun. The children receive backpacks full of books, games, and school supplies. The hope is to provide an exciting, memorable experience for children in foster care, regardless of placement.

Heartfelt Gifts   Our Love Bundles project collaborates with local businesses to provide children in foster care and protective custody with essential developmental items and immediate needs. No matter the season, our Love Bundle backpacks may offer some comfort and necessities to children who have been removed from their homes.

Spring Into Action   Members of our Community Action Committee provide hands-on volunteer service in the community for short-term projects or events. For a spring project, we purchased and built a toddler-friendly outdoor play center for Metropolitan Ministries, a homeless shelter for seventy-five to one hundred children.

Summer Kickoff The Junior League of Tampa conducts a social skills program for students at Academy Prep Center of Tampa, a private, nonprofit middle school for inner-city children. Our volunteers teach the students proper introductions and greetings, table manners, dressing for success, and much more. To finish the school year, we host a special luncheon where the program graduates demonstrate their dining skills.

Fall Festival Members of The Junior League of Tampa act as a special events committee for the Children's Cancer Center, a nonprofit that provides educational, emotional, and financial assistance to children who have cancer or chronic blood disorders. In October, our volunteers host a Halloween Festival for the Children's Cancer Center families. To brighten the faces of children and parents, the event includes everything from pumpkin painting and crafts to a cakewalk and face-painting clowns.

Thanksgiving Feast Our PACE Center for Girls volunteers tutor and mentor students at an alternative school for adolescent females at risk of dropping out of high school. Each November, we host a traditional Thanksgiving feast with turkey and all the trimmings for the girls who may not enjoy a Thanksgiving meal at home.

Season's Readings Our Children's Literacy volunteers read aloud to kindergarten classes in Title I schools throughout Hillsborough County twice a month and provide books for the children to take home. During the holidays, we present each child with a special gift, such as a set of magnetic letters and a holiday book. This has special meaning, because, for some children, the first books we give them are the first of their very own.

CONTRIBUTORS

A special thank you to all of The Junior League of Tampa members, families, and friends who contributed, prepared, and tasted recipes, hosted tasting events, and helped make this book a success. We also thank those whose names we have inadvertently omitted.

Gretchen Anderson	Caroline Burt	Ginger Doherty	Sarah Harrell
Lisa Andrews	Laurie Ann Burton	Alysia Ekizian	Sarane Harrell
Anne Arthur	Julie Byrd	Jeni Eldridge	Nicole Hasselbach
Christy Atlas	Magda Cadet	Gina Evans	Glenda Hauser
Gabrielle Ayala	Liz Caiello	Gina Fair	Susan Hawkins
Lee Ellen Banks	Christina Canody	Leigh Fletcher	Vicki Hayes
Laurie Barlow	Paula Cardoso	Margaret A. Forehand	Rosie Hays
Jean Barrett	Stacy Carlson	Cheryl Fraser	Stacy Heckman
Kristen Barrett	Jennifer Carlstedt	Katherine Frazier	Megan Hernandez
Allison Beard	Maia Chrisman	Sylvia Frazier	Laura Hobby
Allison Belcher	Britton Cisneros	Kimberly French	Glenda Hodgson
Carol Bennett	Jen Cisneros	Laura Darrow Frost	Michelle Hogan
Stacey Bessone	Tracy Clouser	Lisa Gabler	Tara Hoss
Dori Blanc	Marjorie Cochran	Corinne Gaertner	Joelle Hunter
Charlene Bleakley	Rachel Corn	Rebecca Jo Garbrick	Sue Isbell
Lisa Blowers	Marjorie Craig	Sarah Gavlak	Cynthia Janko
Christina Boe	Eileen Curcio	Harrison Giddens	Jennifer Jesski
Susan Boyle	Kathryn Curry	Cristina Godwin	Jennifer Johnson
Becky Brandes	Laurie Daigle	Betsy Graham	Peggy Jones
Allison Brannigan	Tina Dampf	Mimi Graham	Leigh Kaney
Anne Brewer	Shannon Dann	Tara Grigat	Michelle Kaney
Wendy Brill	Kimberly Davis	Jacqueline Griggs	Sandra Kapelowitz
Susan Brindise	Kristen Karig Day	Lynn Guilford	Meagan Kempton
Elizabeth Brooks	Natalie Dean	Donna Hall	Casey Kiser
Greta Brooks	Jennifer Dehnert	Cate Hammer	Lauri Kleman
Chris Holt Brown	Connie Detrick	Kim Harcrow	Suzanne Koutroubis
Helen T. Brown	Pam Divers	Lindsey Hardee	Elizabeth Krystyn
Julie Brown	Terrie Dodson	Sally Hardee	Deanna Laird

Elizabeth Lambert
Trish Lane
Debbie Lawrence
Christina Laxer
Lisa Lockhart
Shannon Longo
Kathleen Lopez
Lee Lowry
Winifer MacKinnon
Jane Maher
Susan Major
Judy Marks
Wilma Martin
Diana Massimini
Erika McCandless
Jessica McIntyre
Jennifer McQueen
Connie Meadows
Nancy Mellon
Suzy Mendelson
Emily Minton
Sarah Beth Morgan
Whitney Moyer
Laura Muldoon
Halle Muntean
Jovanna Nogues
Carolyn Orr
Catherine Pacifici

Sadie Pariseau
Shannon Peifer
Wendy Pepe
Paula Perry
Carolyn Piper
Corey Poe
Anita Popp
Ashley Porcaro
Ashley Prean
Becky Prima
Irene Quisenberry
Amie Ragano
Jane Ramos
Alison Reddick
Christina Roberts
Mariangelica Rojas
Lori Root
Franci Rudolph
Carla Rudy
Ashley Rushing
Kristie Salzer
Catherine Sanders
Gretchen Sebring
Meeghan Seoane
Shelley Sharp
Stephanie Shaw
Meghan Sheil
Taylour Smedley Shimkus

Dori Siverio-Minardi
Kristina Smallwood
Angie Sparks
Susan Steele
Laura Stevenson
Sarah Stichter
Janice Straske
Jennifer Strawser
Heidi Sultenfuss
Marie Sultzbach
Kimberly Tagg
Jennifer Tanck
Julie Tate
Kathleen Thaxton
Amber Thomas
Claudia Thomas
Becky Tolrud
Susan Touchton
Natalie Trudelle
Mary Lynn Ulrey
Lisl Unterholzner
Eliot Van Dyke
Mary Vitello
Leanne Voiland
Christina Volini
Cherie Ward
Lauren Warren
Laura Webb

May Weber
Angela Weck
Missy Weiner
Lisa Weiss
Danielle Welsh
Heather Werry
Kim Whigham
Stacy Williams
Karen Wilson
Lori Wilson
Mary Wilson
India Witte
Lizabeth Wolfe
Laura Woodard
Melissa Yates
Laura York
Erika Zipfel

INDEX

SAVOR *the* SEASONS

The Junior League of Tampa, Inc.
87 Columbia Drive • Tampa, Florida 33606
813-254-1734 ext. 502 • www.jltampa.org

YOUR ORDER	QUANTITY	TOTAL
Savor the Seasons at $17.95 per book		$
EveryDay Feasts at $17.95 per book		$
The Life of the Party at $17.95 per book		$
JLT Culinary Collection at $45.00 (includes *The Life of the Party*, *EveryDay Feasts* and *Savor the Seasons*)		$
The Gasparilla Cookbook at $14.95 per book		$
Tampa Treasures at $19.95 per book		$
Shipping and handling at $4.95 for one book; $2.00 for each additional book		$
	Subtotal	$
Florida residents add 7% sales tax		$
	TOTAL	$

Name

Address

City   State   Zip

Telephone

Method of Payment: [ ] VISA   [ ] MasterCard
                     [ ] Check payable to The Junior League of Tampa

Account Number   Expiration Date

Signature

Photocopies will be accepted.